Walt F.J. Goodridge and www.Passionprofit.com present:
The PassionProfit™ "Websites That Sell" Manual

The author of *Turn your Passion into Profit* presents

The Integrated Life™
a blueprint...

The Passionpreneur™

Websites That SELL Manual

197 proven ideas, strategies and design-tips for creating
an income-generating website for your passion-centered business

Walt F.J. Goodridge

Featuring a special chapter by: Angelo Villagomez

I0463572

197 proven ideas, strategies and design tips for creating
an income-generating website for your passion-centered business
A supplement to *Turn Your Passion Into Profit*™

The PassionProfit™ Websites That Sell Manual (2015)
© Walt F.J. Goodridge. All rights reserved.

Published by The Passion Profit Company, an imprint of
a company called W, New York

The Passion Profit Company
P.O. Box 618
Church Street Station
New York, NY 10008-0618
U.S.A.

Distributed exclusively by
a company called W, dba:
The Passion Profit Company
Available online at
www.PassionProfit.com/store
email: orderdept@passionprofit.com
phone: (646) 481-4238

Retail cost for paperback: $19.95*
ISBN-13: 978-1501032165
ISBN-10:150103216X

Paperback edition printed in the United States of America

Dedication:
This book is dedicated to my grandmother,
Isolene Rebecca Golding
~ before - 1907-1988 - beyond ~

TABLE OF CONTENTS

"Here's what's in store for you!"

All links in the ebook edition of this book are clickable.

SECTION: A CONFESSION

Now that I have your money (or perhaps, now that you've found a way to acquire this book without paying for it*), I have a few confessions to make:

First, this book has way more than 197 tips! I used a smaller number because you might actually have been overwhelmed if you knew in advance that there are actually 262 things to do.

Second, these are more than just things to do. The 262 items include concepts to understand, possibilities to embrace, ideas to execute, anecdotes from my personal experience, case studies of actual websites and webmasters that sell, things to do, and about a dozen separate pitfalls you should absolutely avoid to get and keep your new website making money or to improve an existing one to become a website that sells!

Third, there's no such thing as a website that sells! There are webmasters that sell...who have websites. This manual is about becoming one of those.

*It's never a bad idea to make a contribution/tithe/gift to a seller if you've received benefit--even if you've already paid for the book (Imagine if YOUR own customers did that, eh?); Visit http://www.passionprofit.com/wts/contribute

SECTION: A FEW RECENT TESTIMONIALS

"Here's what people are saying about "Websites That Sell" formula and manual!"

1. ❑ Meet Mel ❑

Mel Catalma hired me to recommend the best platform, install and configure his www.globaltindahan.com website on which he sells products of interest to a worldwide Filipino market. Tindahan is a Filipino word for "store."
"Hi Walt,
The eBay and Amazon strategy worked for me! I started getting orders even before I finished populating my inventory in the X-cart store. From a mere retailer in ebay I became an instant wholesaler. My online sales are soaring by having my own website, and I don't have to share the profit with Amazon!"--Mel Catalma (http://www.GlobalTindahan.com)

2. ❑ Meet Chief Ray ❑

Chief Warrant Officer Raymond was a recent client who had an idea for a unique guide based on his own experience finding employment after two military deployments. The book is entitled Rucksack to Briefcase. Here are two emails he sent--one within 24 hours of us launching and announcing the site (even before the book was written), and the other, a few months later:

"Walt, Received my first sale in less than 24 hours! That's exciting! Can you believe it? My first e-book sale....wow reality in the making."

"hey Walt,
Just wanted to check in with you and let you know how things are going. So far so good. I just did an event this past weekend and the feeling of selling that 1st cash book and the 1st credit card book was awesome. Words can't explain. I know you know. I am working on perfecting my marketing and building a speaking business around the book. I cannot thank you enough for your professionalism, and for holding me to task. I am not sure if I would have completed the project if I did not have you as my coach and mentor. Most of all you are someone I trust, so that helped tremendously. Towards the end when I looked fear in the face--the fear of failure and the fear of success--and just having those stern words from you for me to complete the project, again I cannot put into words. Take care and will keep you posted!"--**Chief Warrant Office Raymond**, author of *Rucksack to Briefcase, a Civilian-Side Job-Hunting Guide for Service Members and Their Families...* Chief Ray's website that sells: http://www.civilianside.com

3. ❑ Get to know Tim ❑

Tim is an online entrepreneur who purchased Websites That Sell. He wrote this review on Amazon:

"Absolute must read for anyone who wants to make a good living on the web! Walt's books are clear, concise, and to the point. No fluff here, just lots of chocolately gooey goodness - you know, the real stuff, no blowing smoke up your butt. He gives you real stuff you can use on how to get your idea on the web and then how to optimize and market it. If you're really serious about making money on the web, this is a great place to start.

"That all being said, Walt has a great number of other books you should check out like Turn Your Passion Into Profit *and* How to Become a Nomadpreneur: an introduction to an uncommon lifestyle. *He even has a great book on relationships called* "If you want to be my girlfriend...": a man's guide to setting standards, living & loving true to your self, getting & satisfying the women you want, all without EVER compromising your masculinity!

"Walt's books changed the way I view life and got me out of my prison of being tied to a company to make money. The point he makes that you could be let go from your company with just one board meeting is right on point - it happened twice to me and it could happen to you. Don't be left out there with no income. Develop multiple streams of income so that you never have to rely on a 9 to 5 job again. Freedom IS achievable!"

4. ❑ Read more testimonials ❑

Visit http://www.passionprofit.com/testimonials

SECTION: REGISTRATION
"Document the journey for future reference!"

5. ❏ Complete the course sign-in & registration ❏

My name is: _____

My Domain name(s): _____

My Passionpreneur identity ("What do I do?"): _____

Product or service: _____

Date started: _____ Date completed: _____

Date my site will go/went live: _____

Date of first sale: _____

SECTION: SUGGESTED PREREQUISITES

"The only way to take control of your life, raise your standard of living and move beyond merely surviving is to create your own unique product or service that you offer to increasing numbers of people in exchange for the things of value that you desire. This simple formula applies to countries as well as people. A self-sufficient economy has its own products or services of value to export to the world. Similarly, a self-sufficient individual has something of value to exchange in the global marketplace. That thing of value is based on your natural talent, skill, or interest—in other words, your passion!"--Walt F.J. Goodridge, author of *Turn Your Passion Into Profit*™

Turning your passion into profit requires a whole new way of thinking and acting. Immerse yourself in PassionProfit™ World by completing these optional, but highly recommended pre-requisites.

6. ❑ Listen to my coaching sessions or workshops ❑

Order the 6-CD audio of Turn Your Passion Into Profit™ featuring live workshops at http://www.passionprofit.com/store/product.php?productid=20

7. ❑ Listen to recordings of interviews I've given ❑

Visit http://www.waltgoodridge.com/interviews (Check out the KY Show Interview, conducted by Skype while I was nomadpreneuring in China!)

8. ❑ Read *Turn Your Passion Into Profit*™ ❑

Order the ebook at http://www.passionprofit.com/store/product.php?productid=1

9. ❑ Read Turn Your Passion Into Profit™ QuickStart ❑

Order the ebook at http://www.passionprofit.com/store/product.php?productid=26

SECTION: THIS MANUAL

"The hardest thing to do in the world--and the hardest skill to acquire--
is to get the human animal to take out its wallet, take out the credit
card and give it to you....very few people have that skill."
--John Carlton as quoted by Eban Pagan, in the Altitude Marketing series

10. ❏ Understand the goal of this manual ❏

The purpose of this manual is to give you that skill. My goal is to empower you with specific tools and techniques so you can bring the things of value you possess (your talent and passion) to an online marketplace successfully and profitably. It focuses primarily on establishing a viable web presence as the basis of your passion-centered business. It is ideal for individuals who have a product or service that people are readily searching for online. (e,g. informational books, CDs, videos, inventions, food products, etc.) and anything that can be delivered digitally or physically with low production and delivery costs.

11. ❏ Commit to using this manual effectively ❏

In this manual, I'm going to share with you website design & layout suggestions, product ideas, marketing strategies and business models I've used to harness the power of the internet to create websites that sell! I'll also share anecdotes intended to underscore specific points I wish to make. Many of the items need to be implemented pretty much simultaneously. Many of the items are ongoing--and need to be revisited at various points in your journey. However, I've arranged them in as close to a sequential order as possible. Here are a few tips to get the most benefit:

(q) To get the most from this manual, never continue reading past a word or phrase you don't understand! It's been shown that the only reason people give up on a new project or course of study is that they encounter a word, phrase or concept for which they have no definition, or the wrong definition I've made an effort to explain words or terms that may be new to you and your understanding of doing business, and there is a glossary in the Appendix. Therefore, if a word in this guide is new to you, please take the time to use the glossary, a dictionary or the Internet to find the most appropriate meaning. This tip is more important than most people know!

(b) Use the checkboxes! (❏) After you've read and performed the necessary activity or are sure you understand its significance, place a check in the box, initial it, place the date next to it, then proceed. Think of this manual as an agreement between your present self and your future self. Your initials represent signing an agreement to live true to your evolving self, your dreams, and your goals. (c) Read this guide at least twice! I encourage you to read the guide once for a general overview, and then again to take notes and action! There's also a second set of checkboxes for your future readings and implementations.

(d) DO NOT skip around or perform the steps in some other order. EXCEPTION: Even though I suggested you proceed in the order I've laid out in this manual, one of the greatest abilities you'll need to master is how to separate unconnected events in order to move forward. I'll give you a simple example:

Most people believe they have to actually write a book before they can sell it. It seems like a logical progression. However, I've learned that those two events--the completion and the selling--are actually unconnected. I can and do, in fact, pre-sell my books, and start collecting money months before a book actually exists--sometimes even before I've written a single word!

Business is full of opportunities like this to move forward in non-traditional, counter-intuitive ways; ways that allow you to get from point "A" to point "D" while filling in points "B" and "C" later on!

Tip: As you move forward, look ahead to the next step and ask yourself "Can I take this next step NOW?" "Do I really need to wait for step 5 to be complete before step 6?" Get in the habit of pushing yourself forward in this way.

12. ❏ Understand what this manual offers ❏

Quite simply, the name of the game in getting website visitors to give you their email address or credit card information to you is called "instilling consumer confidence." Anything you can do to increase consumer confidence in you, your product and your website--along with the value and results each offers--will increase the sales of products or services through your website. I am, therefore, going to provide my most comprehensive checklist of additions, deletions, modifications and strategies you can incorporate into your website and sales pitch to build confidence, improve your rate of sales success and come away with a website that truly sells! Here are a few caveats:

(a) It is impractical to include ALL the information, inspiration and ideas that have contributed to my ability to create websites that sell. There have been books, websites, articles, people I've met, workshops and sales training courses that have all helped shaped who I am. This is important to understand because while there are, in fact, certain tried and true techniques, strategies, headlines and words that can help you create a website that sells, ultimately, your website's ability to "sell" is a direct reflection of YOUR ability to sell. Your website is a mirror that communicates something about you and your product to the world. The more in alignment you become with who you are, what your value is, your purpose on the planet and your identity, the more successful you will be at creating a website that reflects and communicates all of those aspects of your being to others.

Therefore, the secret underlying process that forms the foundation for creating a website that sells is for you to become an entrepreneur who sells. In my opinion, you must embrace a process of personal growth and spiritual development so your website will automatically reflect that in digital form.

(b) You are your own authority--or at least, you will or should seek to become one. In other words, what works for me may or may not work for you for any number of reasons: different product, different market, timing, the reputation of the seller and other factors that affect how a given strategy will actually work in the real world. Therefore, this guide should be seen as a starting point from which to launch your unique online experience and the beginning of a quest to find what works for you, and to become your own authority.

(c) Nothing is written in stone. Everything is changeable. You are not bound by contract or tradition to follow any aspect of these guidelines and suggestions once implemented. As you and your customers and as the internet and its technology evolve, your entire strategy can and probably will evolve, too!

(d) Take your time. Some of these steps may take a few minutes to accomplish (e.g. set up a signature file in outgoing emails), while others may take a few days (e.g. upload and configure your site), while still others are on-going for as long as you're doing business (e.g. compile testimonials, follow up with your customers.) This is not a race to the finish. This is about understanding a new reality, processing the new awareness and incorporating the steps in ways that optimize your understanding. Take the time to understand why each step is important to the overall goal and proceed with what a mentor of mine called "relaxed intensity!"

13. ❑ Make use of the after-purchase support ❑

(a) Email me your questions! (walt@passionprofit.com) I'll respond personally, and your questions will help to improve future editions.

(b) Companies and services I've used in the past have changed, and those I currently use and recommend might change in the future. Therefore, I've placed referral URLs on several specific pages on the passionprofit.com site. I've made mention of these throughout this manual, and they can all be found in the special WTS directory at http://www.passionprofit.com/wts (WTS=Websites That Sell)

(c) Consider purchasing the paperback edition of this manual! Having this information in physical form helps bring the concepts into the physical world. You can tear out individual pages and post on your cubicle wall, refrigerator, bathroom mirror as a constant reminder of the mission you have embarked upon. http://www.passionprofit.com/store/product.php?productid=19

SECTION: ORIENTATION
"What I've learned over the years that might be of value to you!"

14. ❏ Understand how to achieve anything you desire ❏
"Courage is discipline in the face of fear.
Discipline is courage in the face of distraction."

Many people will try to sell you on quick and easy strategies to do just about anything in life--everything from losing weight to making money to having a better sex life. They wish to sell you the magic pill or fairy dust that will work like a charm. Processes may be simple. Specific techniques may be easy. Strategies may work like magic. Certain environments may be more conducive to success. However, what I've found is there is often something missing from these formulas.

It is my belief and experience that you can achieve just about anything you desire in life if you have courage and discipline. It takes discipline to achieve happiness. It takes discipline to make money through a website that sells. That's what it all boils down to. Courage and discipline are the interchangeable, complementary and inextricably linked sides of the same coin. Any solution that suggests otherwise is doing you a disservice.

The good news is you can develop these traits regardless of all the inner and outer challenges you believe you face.

Courage is discipline in the face of fear.

Discipline is courage in the face of distraction.

Once you are introduced to the possibility of a new reality (for example, that you can make money through a website that sells) with different belief system, and a different set of choices, required actions, consequences and benefits, it requires COURAGE to choose to embark on that reality in the face of inertia and fear and habit, society's norms and the opinions of others. Furthermore, once you have actually embarked on the new path, it requires DISCIPLINE to maintain and sustain those actions in the face of inertia and fear and habit and distraction and derision.

To create and sustain a website that sells, you need:
The courage to believe something new about yourself.
The courage to believe something new about how to make money.
The courage to take the action steps to launch your site.
The discipline to keep monitoring and tweaking your websites.
The discipline to keep trying new products and strategies.

The courage to start. The discipline to continue. That, in my opinion, is what it requires to turn your passion into profit with a website that sells! With that understanding, let's continue!

15. ❏ Understand the REAL reason MY websites sell ❏

One of my talents that has been developed into a strength is "creating websites that sell." I've learned how to present myself and products online in such a way that I establish credibility and create enough value for people to pay me money for what I offer. My websites sell (i.e. generate linear income, passive income, royalties and referral income) through the sales and pre-sales of products (books, cds, videos), services (tours, consulting, speaking, logistics), donations & contributions, advertising space.

Over the years, I found myself coming up with ideas for so many websites that I had to develop a process, a system of templates and processes I could use to create these sites and get them up and running as part of my empire quickly.

There's more to this than just effective design. Of course, there are the quantifiable things (good copy, credit card logos, headlines, etc.) that contribute to a site's effectiveness, but there are a other reasons I believe my websites sell:

I am living on purpose.

I am here to "share what I know so that others may grow!" I believe that I am living out my purpose for being here. The products I create are helping me turn my PURPOSE into profit.

I can recognize valuable products

I can recognize valuable products, and I create products and the websites that sell them from the underlying belief that these products have value for others.

For your information, the business that generates the greatest individual sales is my nomadpreneur tour guide venture (a service). My book bestsellers at the moment *are Chicken Feathers & Garlic Skin*, *Fast & Grow Young*, and *Saipan Living*, which are NOT "how to sell on the internet info-products." I mention this because some authors are making the majority of their money selling info-products that show you how to make money online by selling info products that show others how to make money online. These tips and techniques I'm sharing can help monetize service-based as well as product-based businesses that have nothing to do with teaching how to make money online.

I can think like a consumer.

It is a combination of credibility, caring and communication (i.e.
saying the right things, at the right time, to the right people from the desire to improve people's lives.

I've learned what moves people to action.

There's an art to communicating with customers. When I write even the simplest emails, there are certain thoughts and intentions that determine the words I use: *"Give the customer encouragement. Give the customer hope. Make the customer feel good about where they are in their journey. Make the customer feel smart. Share some helpful knowledge and information. Build a rapport."*

Something I learned early on in my sales experience in network marketing is that if I have only 5 minutes to make a sale, I should use 4 minutes and 30 seconds to build rapport, and 30 seconds to ask for the sale!

I can communicate well.

As an author, I've had practice stringing coherent sentences together.

I create the websites myself.

I taught myself HTML back in 1997 and feel comfortable making my own websites, or modifying templates to suit my needs. I can respond quickly to changes that affect my online businesses.

I live it.

I write about and sell what I've personally experienced or achieved.

People can sense my intentions.

I am really doing this to help others. In fact, as if to punctuate that point, a customer named Kyle, just sent me the following message shortly after purchasing the e-book edition of *Turn Your Passion Into Profi*t:

"Hi Walt,

I am currently reading your book: "Turn your passion into profit." I like your philosophy! I believe the saying" like attracts like." I think I'll benefit greatly from your book. It's amazing you are living your passion. I can tell from the words you put into the book. It's really coming from the heart. I love freedom too and hate the 9 to 5 jobs. We think the same but you're ahead. I have much to learn from you."--Kyle

Who you are can be sensed through he words you choose to use whether in your product (like a book), or on your website.

I produce quality products.

Of course, there are a few people on Amazon who might disagree, but for the most part my products are praised for their thoroughness and specificity (albeit with an occasional typographical error).

I'm in this for the duration.

This isn't an experiment for me to "see how it goes" being an entrepreneur. This is my life. This is how I survive and pay my bills. I am a nomadpreneur who earns a living through my websites.

And, finally, my websites sell because I believe they will. I believe (and intend to prove) that it is possible to carve a life of freedom by selling purpose-driven, passion-centered products on the internet.

SECTION: INTERNET PRIMER
"What's needed, plus a little inspiration."

16. ❑ Prepare for the underlying challenge ❑

In order to have a website that sells, you need people to visit your site and perform some required action. There are only three actions a visitor can take upon arriving your website:

1. purchase something
2. sign up to a mailing list, or
3. leave

Your challenge—-to consider your website successful—-is to have your visitor perform either of the first two actions before she does the third! This guide is focused on getting visitors to your site to do just that. Even though signing up to a mailing list is not a purchase, it is just as valuable, because the visitor who gives you his or her email address is also giving you permission to communicate further, which can lead to a future purchase.

17. ❑ Read: How I Made My First Million on the Internet and how you can too! By Ewen Chia ❑

A great resource from an online success story!

18. ❑ Understand the ways your website may actually generate income for you ❑

In some cases, your website that sells will be a stand-alone site, an online store where sales occur, products are downloaded and the transaction and interaction may end there without you ever interacting directly with the customer. In other cases, your website that sells will be the first step--a point of introduction--to an extended interaction face-to-face, by phone, or by email that closes the sale. I've found that the larger the dollar amount of the sale, the more inclined the customer is to want some sort of human contact via email/skype/phone call (at least initially) to build a little trust and familiarity. Thereafter, future large ticket sales (if applicable) are transacted through the site.

19. ❑ Read: *Webonomics: 9 essential principles for growing your business on the world wide web* by Evan Schwartz ❑

I read *Webonomics* in 1998 when I was just beginning my journey online. It helped me understand the basics of presenting products online. Many of the sites used as examples have since been shut down, but the basics of how the internet changed the landscape for selling products remain with me to this day. I think it would be great reading even though a bit dated!

SECTION: YOUR IDENTITY

"In order to create websites that sell, it will be necessary to add new ideas to what you currently believe to be true about yourself, about other people, about the world, and about your role in it."

20. ❑ Take the Passionpreneur Personality Test™ ❑

Your success creating a website that sells hinges on knowing your purpose and passion.

Task: Take my personality test at
http://www.passionprofit.com/itest

21. ❑ Complete the PassionProfit Coaching Questionnaire ❑

I typically provide this questionnaire to my potential coaching clients. It helps me understand a bit more about who I may be working with. It can help you do the same.

Task: View and complete the coaching questionnaire at
http://www.passionprofit.com/wts/coaching

22. ❑ Read: *In Search of a Better Belief System* ❑

"Any belief system that is based on fear, encourages weakness, sanctions intolerance threatens vengeance, promotes passivity and requires you to relinquish your personal power is doing you a disservice." --**Walt F.J. Goodridge**, *In Search of a Better Belief System*

Here is the teaser for the book:

Just because a large number of people believe in a thing, does not make that thing right or make it truth.

People around the world are waking up to that realization as they witness the contradictions, hypocrisy and outright lies in every segment of our society..

We see that those we entrust to guide us spiritually and morally, are themselves spiritually and morally bankrupt.

We see those we elect to lead us selflessly as a society, acting as self-interested individuals.

We see those we expect to safeguard our financial and economic security squandering it freely for their personal enrichment.

We see medicines being sold to the public despite known harmful effects, and those we educate in order to heal us, are knowingly and willfully harming us.

We see those who seek political office legislating based on their own belief systems and agendas and enacting laws despite public opinion and the will of the people they are elected to serve.

Why do we allow these deceptions and betrayals to continue?
We do so because we are trapped in our belief systems. However, a belief system is a choice. Perhaps it's time to make a different choice.

Perhaps it's time to go in search of a better belief system...

Specific beliefs about self, and the world you live in can help you remain focused, stay positive, keep motivated, act in line with your values and ethical code, roll with the punches, recognize opportunities, overcome obstacles, interpret setbacks, decipher clues, keep your own counsel, and create the outcomes and results you desire. Isn't that what a belief system is supposed to do for you?

Download it free at http://www.passionprofit.com/free or
Order the paperback at http://www.betterbeliefsystem.com

23. ❑ Raise your belief level ❑

Even though this is a practical, how-to guide, the key to your success in this or any endeavor is not a matter of logistics but one of belief. In other words the people who will succeed at creating a website that sells are those people who embark on this journey with the belief that it is possible to make money online.

If you do not believe it is possible for you, you can implement all of these steps and still not be successful. Why? Because your belief level affects your thought processes. Your thought processes inform your confidence and creativity which will flavor the types of ideas you come up with, the colors you choose, the words you use, and a whole host of intangibles that will come across through your product and website that can affect your success. In other words, people who "believe" create better products and better websites than people who don't believe.

Anything that you can do, therefore, to raise your belief level will be helpful in improving the quality of the product and website you create, as well as the impact of the words you use to in relation to both. That can include reading about other successes, seeking out and speaking with people who are doing what you wish to do, taking self-help courses, reading and listening to informational and inspirational books and audio.

If you can find someone who's doing it who can coach you, that would be the ideal. I'd love to be able to coach everyone, but since I can't, I'll simply share with you some details about what I have been able to accomplish so that it might help to raise your belief level.

If you haven't already experienced it, the day you make your first internet sale--the day a complete stranger unknown to you enters his/her credit card information on a form on your website or payment page to purchase a product or service from you-- will be glorious day. It will change your belief level.

The day you make two sales in a day will raise your belief level even more.

The day you sell a product that does not yet exist; the day you launch a new website and make your first sale in under 24 hours; the day you earn more than $10,000 in a single sale; all of these are milestones that have a cumulative effect on your overall belief level. These are all milestones I have achieved over the years.

Read other people's success stories. Envision yourself a success. Make it a point to associate with others who share your belief in the liberating power of the internet.

Raising your belief level is an ongoing process. You are never done.

I believe there is so much that has contributed to my ability to create websites that sell--life experiences, attitude, personality, books I've read, people I've met, accomplishments, vocabulary, timing, intuition and the help and well wishes of others.

Mindset is vitally important. Unless you develop a wealth consciousness, you may sabotage your own website's selling power. I've had clients do exactly that. They delay decisions and actions and make and take other decisions and actions that cripple and delay their success.

24. ❑ Read: *Secrets of the Millionaire Mind* ❑

This book by T. Harv Ecker led to an epiphany about a certain money-related experience from my childhood that has affected me all my life, and I now finally have savings (more than one) accounts, contribute to them regularly, and the nature of my thinking has changed to the point where the ideas that come to me are getting me larger chunks of money (e.g. the freesummerconcerts franchise idea came to me as a direct result of reading this book).

25. ❑ Embrace selling...not "shamelessly," but with pride! ❑

People in our society have been led to believe that profit is a dirty word.

I recently read an article about a man who was using Kickstarter (a crowd funding site) to generate 2 million dollars in order to find famed aviator Amelia Earhart's plane.

In the comments section of the article, someone wrote:
COMMENTER 1: "What guarantee do we have he will not:
1) spend 1 million and keep the second
2) steal both millions
3) actually find the plane
4) profit?"

...to which another commenter replied,
COMMENTER 2: "Surely he will profit. But why does that matter? ;)

You see, the first commenter has been led to believe that profit is somehow a bad thing. Yes, why does it matter if the man who finds Amelia's plane profits? If he has committed his time, talents and energy, and as a result, provides a valuable service to the world (and perhaps, to Amelia's estate) why should he not benefit and be rewarded or compensated for his efforts.

I'm always fascinated when I encounter individuals who balk and get turned off when reading website content like this one the moment they realize that something is for sale.

As a "self-help" "how to" author, and as my part of my personal mission, my greatest wish is to share the details of what I've learned with as many people as possible. Therefore, I write books, and yes I SELL those books! That's what I do. That's the VALUE I've been blessed to be able to provide to the world in exchange for the things of value that I desire. That's how I survive. That's how ANY of us survives in this world, really. We offer something of value--whether it's our time, experience, expertise or training--in exchange for money. As a matter of fact, that's exactly what a job is.

If you're working in a job, then you've chosen to sell your freedom--your time, your presence every day in a cubicle or office-- in exchange for a paycheck. Your presence as well as the tasks you perform for your boss are the things of value YOU are selling.
Consider this:

Let's say you work at your job for a week, and at the end of that week, you don't receive your paycheck. Concerned, you walk into your boss' office...
YOU: Hi, Boss, I've given you my time and presence for the past week, but I didn't get paid.
BOSS: Paid??? Yup, I knew it. I KNEW there was a 'catch!' You just want my money! If you REALLY wanted to help me, why don't you work for me for free??? What a scam!

Silly, isn't it? Would you give away YOUR value--your time and presence-- for free? Well, neither would I. It's as if some people think that working a job is noble and acceptable, while selling a product is somehow "shady." People with that belief system will likely remain trapped in a job unless and until they change that attitude.

Furthermore, as long as you have enough money left over for a dinner out and a movie after paying for your rent, food and other necessities, you are, in effect, profiting from your job!

For the record, I absolutely, positively make NO apologies (nor should you) about offering value to the world in exchange for the means to ensure your survival and prosperity. That's what it's all about! That's what turning your passion into profit is all about. That's what living true to your self is all about. That's what creating websites that sell is all about. If you ever want to follow the path that I and others are on, and free YOUR self, you MUST stop thinking that the only "acceptable" way to generate money is as an employee, and expand your self-concept to trade something other than your time and presence at a job in order to earn money. You can never be truly free as long as a single entity controls your income. You can never live true to your self as long as single person other than you decides how much you can earn. You can never create websites that sell as long as you retain an underlying aversion to profiting in any other way.

I recently stumbled upon a kindle authors forum with a thread entitled "Shameless Self Promotion," that encouraged authors to promote their book titles.

I objected to the title of the forum thread. In my opinion, when we allow ourselves to engage in the necessary promotion of our creations, we should do so under a banner heading of PRIDE rather than shame.

According to the dictionary, the opposites of "shame" include "honor, pride, respect" as well as beauty, blessing, delight, enjoyment, esteem, joy, love, treat cherish, dignify, exalt, extol, honor....

I suggest to you that you have nothing to be "shameless" about when it comes to promoting our creations! Instead, be proud! Honor your passion! Respect the value you bring to the table. Shout it to the hilltops!

Using more of those dictionary words, therefore, I'd like to suggest that your creation--your product or service--rather than something to be ashamed about--should instead be acknowledged as a loving and beautiful blessing that provides delight and enjoyment, joy and enlightenment to others, and is an expression of your passion. As such, it should be a source of great esteem--a thing to be cherished, dignified, exalted, honored and extolled to the highest degree! Not something to promote with an underlying feeling of muted shame that needs the approval, validation and permission of others in order for you to indulge.

This feeling of "shame" seems to emanate from a totally contradictory societal ethic that equates the pursuit of sales/money/income by way of self-promotion with something bad--something to feel guilty about. However, in order to create a website that sells, you shouldn't have any qualms about selling your products and services.

This may sound a bit self-serving, but perhaps the first step towards freedom and away from that way of thinking is to honor, respect and purchase from those who are already doing it. You can't envy and begrudge those whom you aspire to emulate and then expect that YOUR path will be easier and that others will honor, respect and buy from YOU when your time for entrepreneurial freedom comes. That single decision and act of generosity and support may be the action that sets you free.

Tip: Become a master seller and never let anyone make you feel guilty or ashamed of making a profit.

26. ❑ Read: *The Science of Getting Rich* by Wallace Wattles ❑

This book is now in the public domain, so there are free copies widely available throughout the internet. There's even an audio version you can download free of charge at archive.org. I've got our own version as well, that I edited for myself and listen to it every day. You can never get enough of these thoughts.

SECTION: YOUR BUSINESS IDENTITY
"Your business has an identity, too!"

27. ❑ Focus on the consumer ❑
People will do just about anything or you...if they like you. There are techniques for building rapport and familiarity and comfort that can translate into the words and images you use to sell your product or service.

28. ❑ Read: *How to Win Friends and Influence People* ❑
This book by Dale Carnegie has probably been the most influential on my interpersonal interaction in both my business and persona life.

29. ❑ Envision your brand ❑
Think about how you'd like to be perceived by the masses.
NOTE: Your brand can change over time.
NOTE: Be careful about who you associate or are associated with. Their brand identity can affect yours.

30. ❑ Read, apply *The 22 Immutable Laws of Branding* ❑
You are always in the process of branding yourself whether you realize it or not. This book helped me understand that everything I do, everything I say, every image on my site--even the absence of an image--contributes to my brand.

By using real-world examples and familiar household brands, the authors explained, illustrated and reinforced the "laws" that govern every aspect of brand-building--from size of niche, size of logo, brand expansion, brand narrowing and more. It helped me fine tune my Passion Profit/Passion Prophet brand and to think of every new product as being part of a brand identity.

31. ❑ Review this Branding Questionnaire sample ❑
Here are my answers for my Hip Hop Entrepreneur™ brand

What is the brand name?
"The Hip Hop Entrepreneur"

What are you branding?
"A resource for information on how to start a record label"

What is the word or phrase that you own?
"Start your own record label"

Who is the target audience, market?
Rappers, producers and hip hop entrepreneurs who wish to release their own music

What's the ONE thing you do?
We help people start, launch and succeed in their independent record label

What are your credentials?
• Had my own record label
• Wrote a book endorsed by Chuck D
• Received hundreds of testimonials from satisfied customers

What category are you the leader in?
Hip Hop Entrepreneur business information

What category question do you answer?
"Will this really help me release my music successfully?"

To see how I incorporated the responses and knowledge gained above into the banner, headline, logo, and web copy, visit www.changethegamebook.com

32. ❑ Complete Branding Questionnaire for YOUR business ❑

What is your brand name? _____

What are you branding?   _____

What is the WORD/PHRASE You Own? _____

Who is the target audience, market?   _____

What's the ONE thing you do?_____

What are your credentials? _____

What category are you the leader in?_____

What is the category question that you answer?_____

33. ❏ Design/create a logo ❏

With what you've learned in *The 22 Immutable Laws of Branding*, you should now get a professionally designed logo for your brand. It doesn't have to be fancy, but it should be consistent.

Remember: nothing is written in stone. Everything is changeable. You are not bound to use this logo forever. Your brand identity can and probably will evolve as you find your true path and calling.

34. ❏ Create a tag line ❏

Widget International. "Where widgets are us"

SECTION: THE BASICS
"There are certain basics you'll need in order to conduct business online."

35. ❑ Prepare the basics of what you will need ❑
(a) internet access
(b) an email account
(c) a business checking bank account
(d) a personal or business credit card or debit card with visa/mc logo for purchases of products/services to get your business up and running
(e) a business/address
(f) social security/tax id number (US based businesses)

36. ❑ Choose the "right" domain name ❑

Now that you've achieved a bit more clarity about yourself and your business, it's time to start laying the groundwork for your online business.

Typically, the very first thing I do with any new project or idea is figure out how we're going to sell it online. So, coming up with the best domain name (your "dot com") is critical.*

WHY: You need a domain name people can spell, remember and share easily with their friends.

NOTE: Sometimes, it might be necessary to purchase a domain name at a premium from a squatter. In order to secure my brand identity, I purchased discoverguam.com for $500 from the individual who owned it. I now own discoversaipan.com, discoverguam.com, discoverpagan.com, discoverbelau.com and discoverchuuk.com—islands in the Pacific with potential for tourism.

37. ❑ Reserve blog name, Facebook page, Twitter account and other social media identities ❑
(example: mybestname.blogspot.com)

38. ❑ Set up hosting account ❑

You can set up a hosting account even if you haven't yet reserved your domain name. This is where your website will exist online.

Hosting with a 1and1.com's "Unlimited" plan is currently $5.99/month (you pay for 12 months in advance), and thereafter is $8.99/month). Go to http://www.1and1.com/?kwk=6837732

However, as my recommendation is subject to change, to find out who I currently recommend for domain registration and hosting, visit http://www.passionprofit.com/wts/hosting.

39. ❑ Request an SSL certificate for your domain ❑

As part of your hosting account features, you'll need an SSL (Secure Socket Layer) certificate. An SSL certificate allows your shopping cart or subscription form (or any page on your site) to be accessed with the URL that includes the "s" in "https" (e.g. https://www.yourdomain.com/checkout.html). This action instructs the cart or form to encrypt and protect any information your customers provide to you. This feature should cost about $49/year.

40. ❑ Set a date for your launch ❑

Give yourself about 30 days to complete this manual, and commit to launching your website by a specific date.

41. ❑ Upload a "coming soon" home page ❑

Once you've got your logo, hosting account and domain name, create a simple "coming soon" page as a placeholder while you create your site.
Suggested content:
"Bookmark this page and check back with us on [date]"
"email us at.........."
"Join our list to be notified of the launch!"
Link to Facebook page
Link to Twitter account
See : http://www.passionprofit.com/wts/comingsoon

42. ❑ Set up your domain-specific email accounts ❑
(eg. orders@domainname.com, questions@domainname.com)

43. ❑ Set up a Paypal™ account ❑

At the same time, you should set up a Paypal™ account. Why? You'll need a way to accept money from your customers by credit/debit card. Go to Paypal.com, get a "Business" account (or choose "Premier" account and upgrade later.) I recommend Paypal at this point because:

- Customers can pay you via Paypal even if they don't have a credit/debit card
- Customers can pay you via credit/debit card if they don't have a Paypal account
- Sales income is immediately deposited into your Paypal™ account
- The debit card gives you immediate access to your funds
- You won't need a "payment gateway" to process orders
- You won't need separate merchant approval from Visa/MC, Discover or Amex
- The fee Paypal™ charges is comparable to—often less than—other processors
- Paypal is more lenient when it comes to approvals of folks with poor credit
- Paypal's business account comes with a "virtual terminal" feature, so you can charge phone-in orders online and won't need a physical terminal (card swiping machine) to charge your customers.
- There is also a new "Paypal™ Here" attachment that connects to your mobile device and allows you to swipe and charge customers in person should you do workshops, conventions and other live, in-person sales events
- Paypal™ can be integrated with a great many number of shopping cart software packages

44. ❑ Integrate a "shopping cart" into your site ❑

If you are selling a single product, you probably don't need a full shopping cart in the beginning. You can use Paypal's "buy now" button to accept payments. However, if you'd like to provide your customers with a customized shopping experience that takes place entire on your site without them being transferred to the Paypal site, you may wish to invest in a shopping cart. You may also choose to start with a shopping cart if you plan to add more products to your site's offering.

FREE OPTION: I've used Cubecart™ , a free option, for many years until just recently.

FREE OPTION: If you use Wordpress as the platform for your site (more on that later), you may also be able to get a free shopping cart "plug-in" for your site.

PAID OPTION: After using MoneyCart™ in the 90s and Cubecart™ for many years, I've now settled on X-cart for their convenient one-page checkout option.
What you'll need for X-cart™ to function optimally:
    (a) Dedicated SSL Certificate; 1and1 provides for $49/year
    (b) a hosting account that supports MySQL database
OTHER PAID OPTIONS: See Paypal's developer site for a comprehensive list of compatible shopping carts, or go to www.passionprofit.com/wts/paypalcarts.html which is a special page I created that will automatically redirect you to the appropriate page on Paypal's developer site.

Remember again: nothing is written in stone. Everything is changeable. You are not bound to use this system forever. Your hosting company, website and order process can and probably will evolve as you find your niche.

Service: If you'd like us to configure, install and optimize your X-cart site for you, feel free to email walt@passionprofit.com

Visit http://www.passionprofit.com/wts/shoppingcart to see who I may be recommending now.

SECTION: YOUR PRODUCT

"If you create and market a product or service through a business that is in alignment with your personality, capitalizes on your history, incorporates your experiences, harnesses your talents, optimizes your strengths, complements your weaknesses, honors your life's purpose, and moves you towards the conquest of your own fears, there is ABSOLUTELY NO WAY that anyone in this or any other universe can offer the same value that you do!"– **Walt Goodridge**

45. ❑ Memorize my favorite definition of a product ❑

PRODUCT: *"a high quality object or service, in the hands of a consumer, in exchange for something of value."*

The important thing to take away from this definition from L. Ron Hubbard's Targets and Goals booklet is that it's not a product until a transfer of value has taken place. It's not a product if it's just an idea in your head or a manuscript that's in a drawer in your desk.

46. ❑ Choose the right product ❑

What is it that you wish to sell? Is it a product? a service? You can sell books, cds, dvds, (plus the electronic, downloadable versions of them), subscriptions, food, toiletries, jewelry & crafts, design services, tour guide services, information, coaching/consulting services, on-the-ground services

Any website that sells also tells the story about a product that sells. It can't be emphasized enough that even a website that sells CANNOT sell a product that doesn't. If your product isn't what people want, then there's no way it will sell even with the best designed and laid out site. My bestselling product at this moment is a book entitled *Fast & Grow Young*. This is an interesting product. All it is is a re-issue of a public domain work now with a new, catchy title. Herbert Shelton wrote a great, but poorly titled book called *Hygienic System Vol III* about how fasting can cure disease and reverse the aging process. I read it and immediately thought a great title would be "Fast and Grow Young," a take off of the popular self-help book, *Think And Grow Rich* by Napoleon Hill. I reformatted the book, added a few extra chapters, and published it on the Amazon, Kindle and Nook platforms. The book is now outselling my previous top-seller, *Chicken Feathers & Garlic Skin*. I've done no advertising or promotion. People are simply finding the book on Amazon and purchasing. A few folks have visited my fastandgrowyoung.com site and then gone to Amazon to purchase.

MORE: See *Turn Your Passion Into Profit*™ chapter on "Product."

47. ❑ Price your product effectively, profitably ❑

a. You are, in effect, in the mail order business. The standard practice is to make your retail price AT LEAST FIVE TIMES the production cost. (e,g. If it costs $2.00 to manufacture your product, you should sell for no less than $10.00.

b. If applicable, set your price on Amazon a little higher. For books in particular, Amazon will usually discount the suggested retail price. Set your Amazon price a little higher so that when Amazon offers a discount, you can match or beat their price without hurting your own profit too much.

c. You should factor in wholesale customers and be sure that if you wholesale your product (typically from 20-55% discount), you can still profit.

d. Sometimes, however, it is necessary to accept that the profit of a particular item may be less or non-existent so that you can sell a higher priced product later. However, avoid selling any product at an actual loss--unless you have the deep pockets to afford it, of course.

48. ❑ Establish a manufacturing and fulfillment strategy ❑

If your product is a book, cd or dvd, you can use Createspace for your product manufacturing. If your product requires factory assembly, food preparation, or other unique manufacturing processes or parts, you can start your search for vendors/suppliers through the Thomas Register Online.
Visit: http://www.Createspace.com

49. ❑ Read: "The Case for CreateSpace™ ❑
Visit: www.saipanpreneur.com/archives/203/

50. ❑ Prepare your product ❑
(a) Imagine/Design your product
(b) Create a sample, mock-up, proof or test version of product
(c) Create your product/service!

51. ❑ Pre-sell your product/service! ❑

You don't need to have everything in place in order to start accepting real money for your product or service. You can start pre-selling at any point. Even your "coming soon" place holder site can generate money for you!

52. ❑ Plan for empire (long term) ❑

What will be the follow-up product? What is the series you can create using this product as the flagship? Is there a real brand of products/services you can create? Start thinking in those terms now!

SECTION:INSTALLATION AND CONFIGURATION

"Here's info on the steps and how much time it recently required for us to get an X-cart-based website up and running for a client. Each case varies."

53. ❏ Review how long it might take to install X-cart ❏

(A) WALT'S ESTIMATE OF TASKS (PRELIMINARY ESTIMATE FOR X-CART INSTALLATION)

1 HOUR	Research X-cart, Bluehost, 1and1 and suggest options
< 1 hour	order and download software
7.0 HOURS	upload x-cart to hosting account
15-20 HOURS	install, configure, set up MYSQL database, and test X-cart software

set up MYSQL database

install software

configure/modify settings as appropriate

design/upload logo

redesign home page as landing page

download/test/generate shipping module if appropriate

configure to work with paypal account; generate cert_key

purchase and install SSL certificate

test software with actual credit card

2-3 HOURS   in-person training session to get up to to speed

BASICALLY, 3-4 days of work

SECTION: YOUR WEBSITE LAYOUT/DESIGN

"Our objective is to create an easy-to-read, easy-to-grasp, easy-to-load website that moves people to take action. There is no mention here of beauty or expense!"

54. ❑ Develop your ability to recognize a good website ❑

If you'd like to develop your ability to intuitively recognize "good" website design from "bad," visit the past tests section of Whichtestwon.com. It shows two test website designs and asks you to guess/intuit/predict which one pulled more sales, got more subscribers, generated more click-through, etc., then shows you the actual results so you can see how good YOU are!
Visit http://whichtestwon.com

55. ❑ Search online for "free website templates"   ❑

Yes, there are sites that offer free templates you can use! Here are two:
http://www.designrazzi.com/category/wordpress-themes/
http://www.1001freewpthemes.com/

FLOW AND ACTIONS

56. ❑ Include a navigation bar on top, side and bottom ❑

The links on the navigation bar do not have to direct your visitor to separate pages. They can link to sections of the same single page. I typically include these links in the navigation bar or in the bottom links on every page:
About Us | About the Founder | Contact Us | Submit Corrections

57. ❑ Get people to the cart as quickly as possible ❑

This works best if your site is, in fact, using a shopping cart as a template. For example, if you use X-cart as your site template, then the product/service information is already contained in a format where an "add to cart" and "checkout" and "buy now" options are clearly visible. The goal is to get people thinking about making a purchase, AND putting them in the environment to do so with the least number of clicks.

58. ❑ Ask for the desired action and make it clickable ❑

"Click here to order" or "To join the mailing list, click here."

59. ❑ Add "Join mailing list" or "subscribe" ❑

Make sure the subscriber/join form is placed prominently, in a different places on site.

60. ❑ Focus on only one or two actions per page ❑

Your visitors should either sign up or purchase. For the same reason as the previous item, you want to limit the distractions and choices you give your potential customer.

61. ❑ Add a "tell-a-friend" form/link ❑

Not essential, but definitely helpful!

62. ❑ Include social network buttons ❑

Addthis.com has a simple code you can add to your site for people to share via Facebook, Twitter, LinkedIn, Google+, Digg, etc.
http://www.addthis.com

63. ❑ Add a survey ❑

People love to share their opinions. Provide the option of participating anonymously, but provide a way for them to opt in to your mailing list too!

64. ❑ Add a donate button ❑

Later, I'll share with you the great success I had with this! (See "My Strategies")

65. ❑ Add a pop-up that evades the pop-up blockers. ❑

"Don't Go Yet" popups are great ways to entice visitors one last time to join your mailing list. The "popup" generated by this code shows up invisibly behind your page, and is not seen until the visitor closes your page. If someone decides to leave your site without purchasing, this little popup will give them one last chance by making a special offer. To see one in action, visit www.passionprofit.com/wts/dontgo. In this example, the name of your popup file is dontgo.html:

```
<script language="JavaScript">
<!—Hide script from older browsers
if(navigator.appName.indexOf("WebTV")==-1){
myWin=open('','winin','toolbar=0,menubar=0,scrollbars=1,sta
tus=0,resizable=1,width=300,height=400');
myWin.blur();
myWin.location = 'dontgo.html';
}
// end hiding contents →
</script>
```

66. ❏ Add a "return to site" link to confirmation pages ❏

After placing an order, or after signing up to the mailing list, your visitor should have the option to "click here" to return to the site.

LAYOUT AND DESIGN

67. ❏ Make the site "responsive" ❏

Your site should be able to "respond" to being viewed on different devices from cell phones to ipads to flat screen tvs. Check out any of my sites and reduce the browser width to see how it adjusts in layout with decreasing size.

68. ❏ Use the long-form web format ❏

Rather than multiple pages layered deep in multiple directions, the most effective website is a single long page that gives the visitor everything he or she needs to know, then calls for an action (subscribe or purchase) at the bottom. I also suggest you use PHP as your coding language.

69. ❏ Fit everything into the top screen shot ❏

By "everything" I certainly don't mean EVERYTHING, but there should be enough information to make a sale. There are always new people coming online and there are still people who don't know how to use the scroll bar at the side of their browser window. It is important, therefore, to include all the information necessary for such a person to make a decision and purchase without ever having to scroll down.

70. ❏ Focus on fewer products per site ❏

Don't confuse or overwhelm your visitor. Most likely, your potential customer has surfed to your site in search of a single item. Sell him/her that single item. More options generally lead to more indecision and confusion. A confused mind is likely to simply shut down and leave your site.

IMAGES & VIDEO

71. ❏ Invest in professional high-quality images, photos ❏

This is an optional step, but one I highly recommend. The images on your site are a very important part of instilling consumer confidence in you and what you do. Blurry, low-quality images will turn your customers off. I typically visit alamy.com and shop for images when designing books.
Resources:
www.123RF.com
www.alamy.com

72. ❏ Choose the best image format ❏

PNGs are almost always superior to GIFs and are usually the best choice. Use GIFs for very small or simple graphics (e.g. less than 10x10 pixels, or a color palette of less than 3 colors) and for images which contain animation. If you think an image might compress better as a GIF, try it as a PNG and a GIF and pick the smaller. Use JPGs for all photographic-style images. Do not use BMPs or TIFFs.

73. ❏ Watermark all your images ❏

Your images should have your domain name watermarked on them so that when people grab them for their own use, it may lead to some exposure for you.
Advanced Tool: Use this tool to automatically add a watermark to all the images in a specific directory.
http://kimbriggs.com/computers/computer-software/perl-image-manipulation.file

74. ❏ Use 3-dimensional image ❏

Include a 3-D picture of product. It's been proven that having an image of your product helps it sell. Further, having a 3-dimensional version of that image increases sales even more.

75. ❏ Design Your Banner and icons ❏

I make sure I use the same color scheme as the product, and include some element of the actual product in the banner. I design my banners in Photoshop. I usually make sure there's a human being in the banner. Consider the following uses for your banner(s) and design different versions based on the required sizes for each use. Each platform may suggest an optimal size, however, I typically make my website banner 900 x 120
Your own website and blog (900 x 120)
Your Createspace™ e-store (760 x 75)

Your affiliates' website
Advertising on other people's sites (determined by site owner)

Design Tools:
Curved Text Logo Generator: http://www.grsites.com/generate/generator/1/
http://www.1001FreeFonts.com
http://dabuttonfactory.com/
Samples: For a great array of banners, visit www.bestofsaipan.com

76. ❑ Use video if appropriate ❑

Videos of you or your product can help customers relate and really appreciate what you're selling in real world terms.

LINKS

77. ❑ Eliminate extraneous outbound links ❑

There are still people new to the internet who think every link on a website is related to that website. You may lose potential customers who may see an interesting Google Adsense link, or a link to your best friend's site and surf away from your page. Don't let that happen

78. ❑ Incorporate adequate white space ❑

Don't clutter your site with fancy bells and whistles or colored background. Having ample white space makes a site look more professional.

79. ❑ Place a phone number in your title tag ❑

That way, the phone number will appear in the title bar of your visitor's browser, showing you've got nothing to hide.

```
<title>The Ultimate Widget--Solve all your problems
overnight! | (646) 481-4238</title>
```

LANGUAGE TO INCLUDE

80. ❑ Lead with customer testimonials ❑

The most powerful confidence builder is what satisfied customers say.

81. ❑ Include third party, industry endorsements/reviews ❑

Again, what others say about you is worth more than you say about you.

82. ❑ Include "in business since..." ❑

Even if your online presence is relatively recent, it helps to put your business age on your site. Of course, if you have no history to speak of—if you just launched yesterday—then this might not be a practical suggestion.

83. ❑ Include the VISA/MC/AMEX/DISCOVER logos ❑

"If they're legit enough for Visa and MC to allow them to put their logo on this site, then they must be somewhat trustworthy!"…or so the subconscious reasoning goes.

84. ❑ Offer Paypal™ as a payment option ❑

In addition to Visa/MC/Amex/Discover logos, place "we accept Paypal™" information just as prominently. (Paypal™ offers a cash back program for purchases made with their debit card as long as you feature the Paypal™ logo on your website)

85. ❑ Offer customers as many options as you can ❑

They should be able to get their product in pdf, paperback, video, kindle, nook, blue color, extra large sizes, etc.

86. ❑ Mention "secure server" for shopping cart ❑

Mention that your customers' information will be safe and secure. The SSL certificate that you purchase as a feature of your 1and1.com account will provide this security. If you are using Paypal for your cart, it's automatic.

87. ❑ Include a privacy statement ❑

Research shows that 40% of customers will read your privacy statement before placing their order. Make this prominent. If possible, you can make it opens in a new smaller window so they don't have to leave the order page.

Sample Privacy Statement:

"We respect your privacy! Any and all the information collected on this site will be kept strictly confidential and will not be sold, reused, rented, disclosed, or loaned!
Any information you provide will be held with the utmost care and will not be used in ways that you have not consented to. If you have any questions, please feel free to call or e-mail us.
Telephone: 1+646-481-4238 Email: orderdept at passionprofit.com"

88. ❑ Include (and honor) a 100% money-back guarantee ❑

89. ❑ Don't forget international customers ❑

Include language to prepare them for additional shipping costs or other pertinent information. If you can translate your entire site into multiple languages, that would be even better!

90. ❑ Add telephone number & support email prominently❑

Worried about being overwhelmed with calls? Don't. most people who are ordering online these days will not switch modalities to pick up the phone. Typically, the occasional calls you receive will be quite manageable. However, a good option is to invest in an eVoice™ telephone number for $4.95/month. This will allow you to be nomadpreneur if you so choose, while still having a number for people to reach you and leave messages.

91. ❑ Mention "bulk sales" if applicable ❑

Remember, the website is just one channel for people to learn about you. It can lead to inquiries from bookstores, colleges and other groups and organizations that wish to purchase.
"For bulk or wholesale orders, please contact us at _____"

TOOLS
92. ❑ Add a tracker code ❑

My favorite is extremetracker.com's free version. You can also access great statistical information using Google Analytics (see Become a Webmaster That Sells)

BELLS & WHISTLES

Many people are tempted to add a lot of what we call "bells and whistles" to their websites—things like flash movies, moving graphics, sounds, music, etc. My firm advice to you is: DON'T!

Remember, you're not creating an entertainment channel. You are creating a website that sells, not a website that sings! In addition, not everyone who views your website is going to have high speed internet access. You should design your site for the least common denominator.

There MAY be a few features relevant to your product or service that you may be wise to add to your site. Think of these as tools or demonstrations to make a point, not dancing bears to entertain visitors. For example, some sensible bells to add to a site might be

- A weather widget added to a tourism site.
- A mortgage calculator to a financial services site
- Rotating images of your product to a fashion or beauty site
- Music to a site selling CDs

Visit Javascriptsource.com for some great scripts which can add some amazing functionality to your site. But, PLEEEEEASE, don't get carried away. Remember, many people still access the web through dial-up connections or using old browsers. Many of these scripts will no work or worse, generate error messages for those visitors.

SECTION: ADVANCED FEATURES, BELLS & WHISTLES

"Here's where I get to show off a bit and share some of the technology and features that have, I believe, increased the functionality, global appeal and overall value and selling power of some of my websites!"

93. ❑ Enjoy this inspiring story ❑

In October 2012, as part of the epiphany and mindstorm I experienced by reading Secrets of the Millionaire Mind, I awoke one day with the idea of taking my freesummerconcerts.com site national. For years, the site was focused exclusively on the New York summer concert scene, but I decided I would expand to include events nationwide, AND involve other webmasters in each state to compile and input the listings of events. However, for that I would need a very unique website.

The site would need to be expandable to 56 states and territories. It would need to have a webmaster's backend so others could input the events for an individual state without affecting the operation of the other sites. It would need to allow webmasters to upload graphics to the server. It would need to recognize cookies as a way to grant access to the

For the next 180 days, I set about creating such a website. I was staying in a relative's empty apartment, with nothing but an air mattress and a card table and a folding chair, so practically all I did each day was work on the computer, sleep rarely, eat barely and spend more time at the computer.

I discovered forums where designers congregated to ask and solve each other's questions. Practically every cool feature/bell & whistle you can think of is doable on the internet. I found little-known code that did almost what I needed it to, and so would have to modify and customize it for my own use. I'd never taken a programming course, so I would have to teach myself how to manipulate php, css, javascript.

There were many weeks where each day after successive day was spent attempting to get one little piece of code to work. I would code, upload, test, tweak, upload, test, tweak, start from scratch, code, upload, tweak and test ad infinitum. It was the most intense design/programming/creative experience I've ever had, and took almost six months from start to finish!

When it was all said and done, I learned how the code to make my site insert cookies into a browser, upload graphics to my server, how to manipulate HTML, Perl, javascript, CSS code to create a unique site that is now doing exactly what I envisioned! From the outset of the project, I knew I was embarking on something unique, so I documented each and every step, each and every resource and forum and email that contributed to the process, knowing that one day I would share it with someone!

The reason I'm so proud of this accomplishment, and why I think it has value to share with you is that even though there are probably thousands of programmers who could code a site like this quicker and more elegantly--the fact is, I don't consider myself a web designer or programmer. I'm simply a guy who doesn't give up until I figure something out! This was a challenge I rose to, met, put my mind to and conquered!

The full details of all the coding and behind-the-scenes functionality would bore you if you aren't among the geekosphere, so the following items in the rest of this section are just a few of the highlights in the form of some great OPTIONAL features that any webmaster--geek or not--will be able to appreciate and find useful in creating a website that sells!

94. ❑ Check out the geopopup script ❑

This little secret popup is something I created that displays a customized, country-specific message to visitors depending on where in the world they are viewing my sites. This involved finding a current list of all IP addresses, creating code to read the ip address of a website visitor, match it against the database, and serve up a country-specific message based on that IP address.
http://www.passionprofit.com/wts/geopopup

95. ❑ Add a time/date stamp or countdown ❑

Adding a script that shows today's date, or adding a script that is counting down to a specific date gives the appearance, at least, that your site is current.

96. ❑ Add a clickable map of the US or world ❑

Visit http://www.freesummerconcerts.com to see it in action!

97. ❑ Allow the public to upload images to your server ❑

This could be a good feature if you are building some sort of community that encourages member participation. See the code at:
http://php.about.com/od/advancedphp/ss/php_file_upload.htm

98. ❑ Customizable Facebook Like box ❑

Visit: http://www.mybloggertricks.com/2011/06/customize-facebook-like-box-with-css.html

99. ❏ On-click Select All ❏
Visit: http://stackoverflow.com/questions/1173194/select-all-div-text-with-single-mouse-click

100. ❏ Texting with Paypal ❏
https://www.paypal.com/us/webapps/mpp/mobile/mobile-text

101. ❏ Send Money via mobile phone ❏
https://www.paypal.com/us/webapps/helpcenter/article/?articleID=94016&m=SRE

102. ❏ Display the number of Twitter followers as text ❏
http://www.bloggertricksandtoolz.com/2011/02/how-to-show-display-number-of-twitter.html
http://www.bloggertipandtrick.net/2010/05/display-twitter-follower-number-as-text.html

103. ❏ Display the number of Facebook followers as text ❏
https://gist.github.com/599243

104. ❏ A simple drop down menu ❏
http://javascriptsource.com/navigation/simple-drop-down-menu.html

105. ❏ Collapsible text ❏
This script allows you to include a lot of information on a page without actually showing that information until the visitor clicks on "show more of this topic." It's a great way to keep the page looking uncluttered. See it in action, along with the code at: http://www.sivamdesign.com/scripts/dwld/col_text.html

106. ❑ An external feed if you don't want to use php ❑

See it in action at: www.saipanliving.com/immigration.html
in the section for Articles from Immigration Lawyers

The Code:

```
<iframe
src="http://www.saipanliving.com/bestofsaipanrightsidebar.php"  //
location of external resource
width="380"  //  width  of  iframe  should  match  the  width  of
containing div
height="283"  //  height  of  iframe  should  match  the  height  of
containing div
marginwidth="0" // width of iframe margin
marginheight="0" // height of iframe margin
frameborder="no" // frame border preference
scrolling="no" // instructs iframe to scroll overflow content
style="
border-style: solid; // border style
border-color: #333; // border color
border-width: 0px; // border width
background: #FFF; // background color
">
</iframe>
```

SECTION: SEARCH ENGINE OPTIMIZATION (SEO)

"Because 'Search Engine Optimization' can be a long-term strategy, it is important to start the process as early as possible in order to yield results in the shortest period of time."

107. ❑ Read the following about the Google Page Rank ❑

It's a bit technical, but useful to know: http://www.webworkshop.net/pagerank.htm
The WebWorkshop site has many more articles about achieving optimal pagerank and search engine position.

108. ❑ Make a keyword list ❑

Before writing your sales copy, make a list of search terms people will most likely use to find your product or service. Here are 3tools you can use to input your keywords to see what variations and phrases people are using to search online. Incorporate these keywords within the body of your website sales pitch.
(a) https://adwords.google.com/select/KeywordToolExternal)
(b) http://www.keywordspy.co
(c) http://www.keywordeye.co.uk
(d) http://www.semrush.com

109. ❑ Add keywords to your keyword meta tag ❑

```
<meta name="keywords" content="practical immortality,age reversal,immortality,how to reverse aging,fit to breed" />
```

110. ❑ Add keywords to your description meta tag ❑

```
<meta name="description" content="How to Reverse Aging-The flagship product of the Ageless Living series of products" />
```

111. ❑ Add keywords to your image tags ❑

People often search for specific images. Therefore, you should have keywords included in your image tags like so: <img src="http://www.mydomain.com/images/palmtree.jpg" alt="photo of palm tree, coconut tree" title="Palm tree on beach" width=300 height=100>

112. ❑ Become a webmaster that sells! ❑

Visit http://www.googlekeywordtool.com/ for links to other webmaster resources

SECTION: YOUR WEBSITE SALES COPY

"The most important part of creating websites that sell is what you say, how you say it, and to whom you say it. In this next section, you will develop a winning headline, sales copy, testimonials, and more of the words that are required to move people to action."

113. ❑ Use second person voice ❑

Speak to the customer as "you."

114. ❑ Create a winning headline ❑

Some people start with the headline. Others gather all the information first and then do the headline last. Tip: I often like to include an action word in my headlines (i.e. Order, Buy, Get)
MORE: View http://www.passionprofit.com/wts/300bestheadlines
for a list of idea-generating headlines that has been online for over 10 years!

115. ❑ Collect testimonials ❑

If anyone has happily used an early version of your product or service, contact them and request a testimonial. If you've received testimonials over the phone or in person, contact those people and take dictation.

116. ❑ Visualize your ideal prospect/customer ❑

Create a profile of your ideal customer. Male or female? What age? What level of education? What specific challenges or situation are they in that are relevant to the product/service you are offering? Once you create this individual in your mind, you should keep them in your mind's eye as you write your copy and pretend that you are speaking directly to that person.

117. ❑ Relate to your prospect ❑

What do you and your prospect have in common? What experiences, philosophy or worldview do you have in common? Talk about that!

118. ❑ Understand what moves people to action ❑

Use the language of motivators in your sales copy. People are moved to action by (a) Money, (b) Fun, (c) The desire to help others, (d) Facts and documentation; credibility; status

119. ❏ Use the following words in your sales copy ❏

Therefore, if the purpose of your website is to elicit some sort of action, then your sales copy should include references to making money, having fun, helping others, in addition to the statistics, etc

☐ Include the following words in your sales copy

☐ free	☐ guarantee	☐ quick
☐ proven	☐ easy	☐ offer
☐ you	☐ hurry	☐ now
☐ suddenly	☐ remarkable	☐ compare

120. ❏ Use keywords in your sales copy ❏

Sprinkle the keywords you compiled in an earlier step throughout your sales copy.

121. ❏ Use "fear of loss" ❏

People are moved to action more by what they stand to lose rather than what they stand to gain. ("Act now, or miss out on this special offer!" "Use this product today, or lose your hair tomorrow!") Include compelling reason(s) to seize the opportunity today!

122. ❏ Use the Web Copy tool to write your sales copy ❏

Starting with the compelling headline, using the answers to the brand questionnaire, speaking the language of motivation, invoking the fear of loss, sprinkling in keywords, answering the killer web copy questions, you can now write your compelling sales copy!

(a) Who are you and why should I trust you?
Include compelling reason(s) to believe that what you say is true.

(b) Why did you create this product?

(c) Who was it created for?

(d) What problem does the product solve, and for whom?

(e) How long has the product been selling steadily, and why?

(f) What uses or occasions is the product especially appropriate for?

(g) Where would you normally find one of its ingredients or components being used?

(h) What DOESN'T the product have that makes it superior?

(i) What DOES the product have that makes it superior?
Include a compelling reason(s) why your product is superior to other solutions your prospects might choose, including doing nothing.

(j) It's a cross between a what and a what?

(k) What does this product go well with?

(l) What kind of testing went into making the product?

(m) Why is the price so reasonable?

(n) Why might you want more than one product?

(o) How will the user feel when (or after) using it?

23. ❑ Add something timely and relevant ❑
Find some news item that you can incorporate into your copy or headline. Be careful, however, not to get too political, as that may affect your sales by creating factions within your audience. If there's a recession in effect, some special holiday coming up, some news event, the Olympics, or some other major event or happening that can add a timely image to your site, then incorporate it! (Don't forget to update your site once the timely event has passed)

124. ❑ Write a short and long-version product description ❑
Write a 56-character summary, a 20-word summary, and a one line summary. These different length product summaries will be used for various types of sites, listings, articles, etc.

125. ❑ Write a short and long-version author/founder bio ❑
Write a 56-character summary, a 20-word summary, and a one line summary. These different length product summaries will be used for various types of sites, listings, articles, etc.

126. ❑ Use everything above to create your press release❑
(For samples, see Appendix)

127. ❑ Make sure spelling is correct ❑

Some of your customers will forgive you—especially if they themselves can't spell—however, those who can may be turned off by obvious grammatical errors and misspellings (Um, did I spell misspellings correctly?)

SECTION: INITIAL LAUNCH & TESTING

"This section is especially important if you've created a website using your own html/php code. However, if you've used Wordpress or X-cart as your site template, then many of these tweaks have already been incorporated into the basic design, OR can be integrated with simple adjustments to the Wordpress or X-cart dashboard.

128. ❑ Upload your site ❑

Using your ftp client (Fetch, FileZilla), upload your site and images to the internet. (Make note of the date your site has "gone live" in the registration section of this manual)

129. [] Test for HTML compliance []

One of the first things I do if I'm designing my own site is to test that my HTML code is perfect. Use the tool at http://validator.w3.org to make sure your html is error-free and will resolve correctly in the current browsers. It will also correct the HTML code for you! Great stuff!

Visit: http://validator.w3.org

130. ❑ Test all links ❑

This probably goes without saying, but like most things that "go without saying," it probably needs to be said: make sure you test all the links on your site, and go through the entire order process as if you are a visitor and customer of your site.

131. ❑ Test how your site appears on multiple devices ❑

Of course, the best way to be sure is to test your site on an actual mobile phone. However, here are some emulators that can help.

http://iphonetester.com/

http://www.mobilephoneemulator.com/

http://ipadpeek.com/

SECTION: SECTION: TESTING FOR SPEED
"Everyone wants a fast-loading website!"

132. ❏ Test your site for speed ❏
These are great tools for testing how fast your website loads!
(a) http://tools.pingdom.com
(b) https://developers.google.com/speed/pagespeed/insights/
(this tool shows how your site will appear in mobile devices as well as laptops)
 (c) http://gtmetrix.com
This great tool tests your site's speed and gives specific instructions
on how to improve it. The following tips are from a typical GTmetrix analysis;
they may be a little advanced for those who are not familiar with HTML, CSS and
web design in general.
You can find more detailed explanations at
https://developers.google.com/speed/docs/best-practices/payload?csw=1

133. ❏ Add compression code above header ❏
Compressing resources with gzip or deflate can reduce the number of
bytes sent over the network. The following code added to the top of your php
page will help the page load faster.

```
<?php if (substr_count($_SERVER['HTTP_ACCEPT_ENCODING'], 'gzip'))
ob_start("ob_gzhandler"); else ob_start(); ?>
```

134. ❏ Test if your Gzip code is working ❏
http://www.gidnetwork.com/tools/gzip-test.php []

135. ❏ Remove unused CSS code ❏
Removing or deferring style rules that are not used by a document avoid
downloads unnecessary bytes and allow the browser to start rendering sooner.

136. ❏ Minify Javascript, CSS and HTML ❏
Compacting JavaScript, CSS and HTML code can save many bytes of data
and speed up downloading, parsing, and execution time.
This tool compresses Javascript: http://jscompress.com/
This tool compresses HTML code: http://htmlcompressor.com/

137. ❑ Test if your site's compression code is working ❑
http://www.whatsmyip.org/http-compression-test/

138. ❑ Defer Javascript (i.e. place at bottom of page) ❑
Deferring loading of JavaScript functions that are not called at startup reduces the initial download size, allowing other resources to be downloaded in parallel, and speeding up execution and rendering time.

139. ❑ Optimize images ❑
Many software programs allow you to reduce the resolution and thus the file size of an image. This helps the image load faster.

140. ❑ Use an appropriate image file format. ❑
As mentioned earlier, PNGs are almost always superior to GIFs and are usually the best choice. Use GIFs for very small or simple graphics (e.g. less than 10x10 pixels, or a color palette of less than 3 colors) and for images which contain animation. If you think an image might compress better as a GIF, try it as a PNG and a GIF and pick the smaller. Use JPGs for all photographic-style images. Do not use BMPs or TIFFs.

141. ❑ Specify exact image dimensions ❑
Your image code should look like this <img src="http://www.domain.com/image/me.jpg" width="200" height="200" alt="an image of me" title="this is an image of me">

142. ❑ Serve scaled images ❑
If your webpage layout calls for a 200px by 200px image as above, you should create the actual image at that size.

143. ❑ Place CSS code inline ❑
Place CSS code within the web page code rather than in an external file.

More: https://developers.google.com/speed/docs/best-practices/payload?csw=1

144. ❑ Reduce external references ❑

You should reduce the number of links that take the visitor away from your site, as well as links to content (images for example) that reside on different servers. You should serve these resources from a consistent URL. This practice also helps with your SEO ranking.

145. ❑ Test in different browsers ❑

Make sure your site is viewable in Safari, Netscape, Internet Explorer, Firefox and any other browser your familiar with.

146. ❑ Look at my speed test results to see it works! ❑

When I first tested my sites for speed, I was scoring in the 60s and 70s. I had to do something! I set my goal for between 90 and 100, and got to work making the changes above. My scores shot up after I implemented a few of the suggestions above. The biggest jump came when I moved my CSS code inline.

	BEFORE		AFTER MAKING CHANGES	
	gtmetrix	*pingdom*	*gtmetrix*	*pingdom*
passionprofit	67/100	86/100	AFTER: 96/100	98/100
destinationsaipan	72/100	83/100	AFTER: 93/100	95/100
discoversaipan	71/100	90/100	AFTER: 94/100	90/100
waltgoodridge	75/100	82/100	AFTER:	
hiphopbusinessplan	73/100	90/100	AFTER: 90/100	95/100
hiphopbiz.com	75/100	97/100	AFTER: 97/100	96/100
fittobreed.com	67/100	86/100	AFTER: 83/100	92/100
dexterstyle.com	70/100	89/100	AFTER: 97/100	97/100
coffeepotcookbook.com	67/100	89/100	AFTER: 97/100	92/100
changethegamebook.	74/100	84/100	AFTER: 87/100	96/100
agelessadept.com	63/100	93/100	AFTER: 96/100	98/100
betterbeliefsystem.com	79/100	86/100	AFTER: 90/100	95/100
taoofwow.com	79/100	89/100	AFTER: 98/100	93/100
saipanliving.com	71/100	82/100		
saipanfactorygirl.com	68/100	82/100	AFTER: 85/100	94/100
livingtruetoyourself	79/100	89/100	AFTER: 96/100	100/100

Note: scores may vary slightly depending on where the site is tested from

147. ❑ Seek out support ❑

If you are very technically inclined and do your designs yourself, you can often find great support at http://stackoverflow.com/questions These are also helpful for speeding up your site:
http://www.askapache.com/hacking/speed-site-caching-cache-control.html

SECTION: BECOME A WEBMASTER THAT SELLS
"A website that sells starts with a webmaster that sells!"

148. ❑ Join and participate at Webmasterworld.com ❑
Ask questions, and share information in forum discussions
http://www.webmasterworld.com

149. ❑ Visit and join the ProBlogger.net mailing list ❑
http://www.ProBlogger.com

150. ❑ Start a Google Webmaster Tools account ❑
http://www.google.com/webmasters/tools

151. ❑ Start a Bing Webmaster account ❑
http://www.bing.com/toolbox/webmaster

152. ❑ Set up a Google Analytics account ❑
https://www.google.com/analytics/

SECTION: MARKETING, PROMOTION & PUBLICITY

"The prime directive of your publicity, marketing and promotion efforts should be to drive traffic to your site in order to build familiarity, credibility, believability, trust and desire for your product in the minds of your potential customers."

153. ❑ Understand and implement Non-Existence Formula ❑

I'm following a series of formulas explained in Turn Your Passion Into Profit. Starting with the Non-Existence formula which is applicable for new projects and new

a. Find the Lines of Communication
b. Make yourself known
c. Discover what is needed or wanted
d. Produce or deliver it

Note: If your site is already selling products, a different condition formula may apply to you. See Turn Your Passion into Profit for details on how to determine which condition formula applies to you.

154. ❑ Find the lines of communication ❑

Your communication lines are simply the people, organizations, contacts, potential customer pools and anyone in your industry who should know about you and your product. Making a list of these "comm" lines will help you to tailor your sales pitch effectively and to the right audience. Start with your friends and social network. Include every person, entity, organization, magazine, corporation, media outlet that is relevant to your product or service.

155. ❑ Make yourself known ❑

Once you've determined your lines of communication (this is an ongoing process), the next step is to make yourself known. Contact them, to let them know you exist. This can be done with an email or a press release.

156. ❑ Discover what is needed or wanted ❑

In the process of contacting and interacting with your communication lines, you need to discover what they need from you in order for both of you to do business with each other. In many cases, we already know what is required: magazine editors need timely and informative articles and press releases. Bookstores need books that sell; clubs and organizations need products that may help their membership achieve their goals. Google wants well-designed websites with valuable content (and a sitemap is helpful). The best way to find out what your customers want is to survey them. You can create and post a survey on your site using http://www.surveymonkey.com

157. ❑ Produce or deliver it ❑

Once you know what your communication lines and/or customers need or want, your next task is to produce it and deliver it!

With that said, let's start to implement producing what is needed! You've already produced a website that sells. Next are a few tools for promotion and exposure.

158. ❑ Create a sitemap ❑

According to sitemaps.org: "Sitemaps are an easy way for webmasters to inform search engines about pages on their sites that are available for crawling. In its simplest form, a Sitemap is an XML file that lists URLs for a site along with additional metadata about each URL (when it was last updated, how often it usually changes, and how important it is, relative to other URLs in the site) so that search engines can more intelligently crawl the site."

X-cart shopping cart has a "create sitemap" option as part of its modules. However, you can create
a sitemap using the following tool on my site:
http://www.passionprofit.com/wts/sitemapgenerator.html

159. ❑ Write press releases ❑

For guidance writing a compelling press release, see sample press releases in the appendix.

160. ❑ Write articles ❑

Not everyone can be (or wants to be) a writer. However, it never hurts to have at least one article to your credit that can be used online to generate traffic to your website. It can simply be a "Top 10 Things That...." type of article that is relatively easy to assemble.

Next, let's start delivering it! Remember, your goal is to be seen, heard and talked about in as many outlets as possible.

FREE OPTIONS

161. ❑ Register your site URL and sitemap with Google ❑

According to research, 76% of online searchers click only on the natural search results, as opposed to the sponsored/paid results. What this means is that you MUST have some strategy to appear in the regular listings or you will be missing out on a great percentage of visitors to your site.

Log in to your Google Webmaster account and submit the site URL and sitemap.

162. ❑ Submit URL and sitemap to other search engines ❑

Most of the major search engines (Google, Yahoo, Bing, AOL) "crawl" and "spider" the web on a regular basis and will index your site without you having to do much. However, it won't hurt to use a free service to make sure it's added to some of the lesser known search engines. There are dozens of search engine submission services.

OPTION: Use Submitnet.net or http://www.addme.com to register your site with 200 search engines (Look for their 90 day free offer);

163. ❑ Announce site/product to warm market & lists ❑

Your "warm" market includes friends, associates and those with whom you have a closer (warmer) relationship.

164. ❑ Submit press releases ❑

Use a press release distribution service to announce your company/product to the industry and to the world. Many of these services have free as well as paid options.

Here are a few:

http://www.prweb.com
http://www.PrLog.org
http://www.PR.com
http://www.TheOpenPress.com
http://www.IdeaMarketers.com
http://www.I-newsire.com
http://www.Newswiretoday.com
http://www.Free-Press-Release.com
http://www.24-7pressrelease.com
http://www.EcommWire.com

165. ❑ Submit articles to distribution/aggregator sites ❑

Here are just a few:
http://www.ezinearticles.com
http://www.findarticles.com
http://www.yahoogroups.com

166. ❑ Finance/publicize your project with Kickstarter ❑

Crowd funding sites like Gofundme and Kickstarter are great places to publicize your site if your product or service is appropriate.
See http://www.kickstarter.com/projects/1116206143/love-peace-and-sooouuuul-americas-favorite-dance-s for a great example of a Kickstarter campaign

More: International list of crowdfunding sites: http://en.wikipedia.org/wiki/Comparison_of_crowd_funding_services

167. ❑ Become a HARO expert ❑

HARO stands for Help A Reporter Out. This free service posts requests from reporters/editors/writers who are looking for experts for a given subject. Visit: http://www.haro.com

168. ❑ Do guest blog posts ❑

Posts to blogs that offer related content and begin to build your expert credentials in a given category or niche.

169. ❑ Request reviews of your products on Amazon, etc. ❑

If there are high-traffic sites on which your products are selling, ask your friends, family and customers to post reviews on these sites.

170. ❑ Request reviews and links from related sites ❑

Request linkbacks preferably from PR4, 5, & 6+ sites

171. ❑ Answer questions on expert sites* ❑

* Be careful about being too accessible. By this I mean you should be aware that if your posts and comments on other sites are too plentiful, it gives a particular impression about who you are. This may or may not be a bad thing depending on what type of brand identity you wish to cultivate for yourself. Are you a

neighborhood expert who is always posting on sites? Are you an international guru or entrepreneur who simply is too busy and inaccessible to have time?

172. ❏ Post to bulletin boards* ❏
* Be careful about being too accessible. See above.

173. ❏ Comment on articles in your field* ❏
* Be careful about being too accessible. See above.

174. ❏ Add to wikipedia, wikitravel, et.al. ❏

Have someone other than you add mention of your product/service to relevant wiki page. It could be wikipedia, wikitravel, or any of the multitude of wiki sites that exist. My book, *Chicken Feathers and Garlic Skin: Diary of a Chinese Garment Factory Girl on Saipan* was added to a wikipedia.org page about Saipan and one about sweatshops. Follow the wikipedia rules that frown on self-promotion.

COMMUNITY "BUZZ" BUILDING

175. ❏ Start and grow a mailing list of email subscribers ❏

176. ❏ Start and grow a forum community ❏

177. ❏ Start and build a Twitter following ❏

178. ❏ Start and grow a Facebook group ❏

179. ❏ Set up YouTube channel ❏
Post videos on YouTube linking back to your site

180. ❑ Keep up with the latest social networks ❑

Whether it's Myspace, Google+, Digg, Instagram, Tumblr, etc., there seems to always be a new social network popping up often.

OTHER BUZZ BUILDING STRATEGIES

181. ❑ Add a signature file to your outgoing emails ❑

182. [] Create a short kindle ebook (sell for $0.99 or free) []

Marketing Tip: Include a link to your website in your product description and at the very top of your kindle ebook.

183. [] Read what works for me []

I give something away free. It's a no-brainer, but giving something for free drives traffic to your site. I have several "free strategies" that I use.
(a) I have a free personality test on my passionprofit.com website.
(b) I have a free site, freesummerconcerts.com, that I use to expose people indirectly to my products
(c) Usually, my sites offer free chapter excerpts, audio downloads for potential customers to sample.

A FEW PAID STRATEGIES (ADVERTISING)

In time, if your site is optimized as I've suggested, you will naturally start to get traffic as people search for what you are offering. However, here are a few options for speeding up the process of people knowing about your website:

184. ❑ Set up Google Adwords™ account ❑

Use Google's Adword Program to launch a keyword ad campaign
- No money is needed INITIALLY to start the campaign.
- You pay only for clicks received, possibly as little as 5 cents per click.
- Your credit card will be billed at the end of the month.

185. ❑ Place classified ads in college newspapers ❑

Of course, you can place ads in local newspapers, pennysaver-type magazines, newsletters and just about anywhere. I've suggested college newspapers because their rates tend to be cheaper.
List of college newspapers in the US you can contact:
http://en.wikipedia.org/wiki/List_of_student_newspapers_in_the_United_States

SECTION: PRICING STRATEGY
"Price your product for profit. Base it on the value you offer!"

186. ❑ Resolve to NEVER compete on price. ❑

Do your best NOT to compete on price. In other words, do not attempt to gain customers by charging less than your competition. It's a no-win race to the bottom. Remember: there is always someone somewhere who can undersell you. There will always be websites that can charge less for a product that is perceived to be the same. Your mission is to make your product/service stand out as unique, and you should be highlighting the unique selling proposition(s) of your product or service so that people will WANT to (or at least not mind if they have to) pay more for it.

Of course, this strategy is not always possible, for instance if Amazon is selling the same book you are. However, you might try adding value to your offer (e.g. order from us and we'll throw in an extra widget or a free wadget, or give you an autographed copy!)"

187. ❑ Read: No. B.S. Marketing to the Affluent ❑

Conflicted about charging more for your product or service? Author Dan Kennedy will slap you into a profitable, common-sense reality!

SECTION: SALES STRATEGY

In some cases, your website that sells will be a stand-alone site where sales occur, products are downloaded or shipped and the transaction and interaction may end there. You may never interact directly with the customer. In other cases, your website that sells will be the first step--a point of introduction--to an extended email or face-to-face interaction that closes the sale. I've found that the larger the dollar amount of the sale, the more inclined the customer is to want some sort of human contact via email/skype/phone call (at least initially) to build a little trust and familiarity.

188. ❑ Read what works for me for generating LINEAR, RESIDUAL website income ❑

(a) The most single-day sales I ever received for my book, Turn Your Passion Into Profit™, came after a review in the Dallas Morning News newspaper. People ordered directly through my site.
Check out the article here: http://www.passionprofit.com/wts/dallasnews

(b) The second best strategy for generating sales is an endorsement from a person with a following who is perceived as credible within a particular industry or region. I noticed an increase in sales when Angelo Villagomez (the Saipan Blogger) recommended *my Chicken Feathers and Garlic Skin: Diary of a Chinese Garment Factory Girl on Saipan*, and my *Jamaican on Saipan* books. (ordered primarily through Amazon)

(c) Similarly, when David B. Cohen, Former Deputy Assistant Secretary of the Interior for Insular Affairs recommended *Chicken Feathers and Garlic Skin* on his Facebook® page, there were increased sales as well. (through Amazon)

(d) When another music industry site with greater traffic carried my Hip Hop Entrepreneur® products, we made more sales and split the revenue).

(e) The greatest single transaction sale I achieved through my website (over $10,000) was for organizing an expedition to the remote, pristine island of Pagan (pronounced PA'gan) through my DiscoverPagan.com site. See more details about that in Nomadpreneur SECRETS!

189. ❑ Read what works for me for generating PASSIVE income through my website ❑

The Adsense™ text ads on some of my sites generate regular income. This strategy fluctuates, but generally works well when I focus on it.

190. ❑ Read what works for me for generating CONTRIBUTION income through my website ❑

The seasonal site, FreeSummerConcerts.com provides a particularly good stream of income for several months during the year.

SECTION: MONITORING YOUR SITE

"Your site is up and running. You're doing all the right promotion activities to get visits to your site. You need to know who visits your site and shopping cart, when they visit, and where they are located."

191. ❑ Track visits to your website ❑

Visit the results page of the public tracker you installed during the design/layout process. Make note of what keywords people are using to find you. Make note of what states or countries your visitors are coming from. If you are using PHP as I recommended, you can also add this bit of code to the top of your site home page. It sends you an email whenever someone visits your site. Keep in mind that search engine spider visits to your site will also activate this bit of code.

```
<?php
$ip2=$_SERVER['REMOTE_ADDR'];
$referer=$_SERVER['HTTP_REFERER'];

$message1 = "Someone visited my  home page";
$message2 =" IP Address= http://www.ip2location.com/$ip2\n
REFERED BY= $referer\n
";
$to = "you@yourdomainname.com";
$subject = "$message1";
$message = wordwrap($message2, 70);
mail($to, $subject, $message);
?>
```

Test it out! Add the code to your homepage. Change "you@yourdomainname.com" to our email address. You'll notice that this code also grabs the visitor's IP address and included a link to a site for you to see where that IP address is located!

192. ❑ Track clicks to shopping cart and checkout ❑

I've added that same bit of code to my X-Cart shopping cart to sends me an email whenever someone visits the shopping cart, adds an item to their cart and proceeds to checkout. This helps me see, in real time, what is happening on my site, and allows me to respond quickly if someone abandons his/her cart and fails to place an order. It also tells me which pages/sites are referring my products. This also helps me spot any broken/old links in my websites.
Contact us for help setting up such a script.

193. ❑ Proceed, adjust course, rinse & repeat! ❑

Remember: Launching and monitoring your website is an ongoing process. You'll constantly be incorporating feedback and suggestions on how to improve your customers' online experience.

SECTION: YOUR MAILING LIST

"Email addresses and the permission to use them are just as valuable as a direct sale. In fact, it may be more valuable than a single sale because you will then have a constant line of communication through which to sell more and more valuable products/services."

194. ❑ Set up a list management system ❑

The Wordpress platform provides many mailing list management options. You can also use a third party service like Mailchimp. (I've not used Mailchimp, but they've got a memorable name!)

195. ❑ Set up an auto-responder system ❑

One of the most powerful ways in which I've automated my system is to have "autoresponders" for communicating with my mailing list. Using my own customized software (off the shelf versions are readily available; see http://www.passionprofit.com/wts/autoresponder for which service/software I currently recommend), an autoresponder allows me to pre-program specific messages that will automatically be sent to anyone who subscribes to my mailing list. For example, if John joins my list on Monday, he will receive message #1 on Tuesday, message #2 on Wednesday, and so on. If Susan joins my list on Tuesday, she will receive message #1 on Wednesday, and message #2 on Thursday, and so on. This system guarantees that everyone will be taken through the same sequence of communication regardless of when they join.

Search for auto responder from your wordpress dashboard.
Visit http://www.passionprofit.com/wts/autoresponder

196. ❑ Implement "Bulk Senders Guidelines for Gmail" ❑
Source: https://support.google.com/mail/answer/81126

The challenge with communicating through a traditional email list is making sure emails get through to your subscribers. Spam blocking algorithms make it harder and harder for legitimate email messages to get through.

197. ❑ Include product link in all outgoing emails ❑

198. ❑ Communicate regularly with your Facebook groups and Twitter followings ❑

In this new era, Facebook groups and twitter followings have almost replaced email lists.

199. ❑ Communicate regularly with your email list ❑

Even beyond the autoresponder messages, you should make an effort to communicate directly about current events and newsworthy items with your mailing list. Don't rely exclusively on the autoresponder.

200. ❑ Blog regularly ❑

And speaking of blogging, here is a bonus chapter:

SECTION: BONUS CHAPTER ABOUT BLOGGING
BY ANGELO VILLAGOMEZ

"Blogging is a great, methodical way to build content over time. An entry a day starts to build the content that's available for searches. Search engines place a higher priority on sites that have relevant content. So, as traffic increases, clicks on your ads and purchases of your product are bound to increase.

"My friend, Angelo Villagomez, introduced me to the world of blogging. Here is a special chapter he's written just for Websites That Sell!"

10 EASY STEPS TO BECOME TOP BLOG
by Angelo Villagomez, The Saipan Blogger

Want a ton of Internet traffic? Just be sexy, intriguing, and controversial. If only it were that easy.

On Wednesday August 8, 2007, I checked my blog stats and noticed that somebody had found my personal blog, The Saipan Blog (http://www.thesaipanblogger.com), by doing a Google search for "Most Popular Blog Ever." I wondered how high my blog was on such a search, so I opened up Google, typed in the phrase, hit enter, and there I was, sitting atop 90,600,000 other search results.

I've read that there are now over 100 million unique blogs, so how did Google come to rank me as the "Most Popular Blog Ever?" Well, I think I have an idea…but before we go there, let me just introduce myself.

My name is Angelo Villagomez, I am 28 years old and I live on an island in Micronesia called Saipan. Google my name. You'll find that I'm an environmentalist and that I publish to about 15 different blogs. I don't sell anything on my blogs. I use them to keep friends and family around the world up to date on what I'm doing and to promote my different environmental activities and pastimes, like playing soccer, taking photographs, reading, and eating.
Some of my blogs, but not all of them, have Yahoo Publisher ads, and my personal blog, The Saipan Blog, has exactly five posts with some self-negotiated pay per post advertising.

So far I've made just over $100 per month in 2007. This is passive income. This is money I make while telling my family what I'm doing in Saipan. This is revenue I generate while I'm doing my real job and in my sleep. Not bad for a hobby, ne?

I was asked by Walt Goodridge, a fellow Saipan resident, to write a chapter for his upcoming ebook Websites That Sell. (I wonder if he sees the irony in asking someone who has never sold anything on the Internet to contribute to a book with that name?)

Anyway, I found out about Walt online. He moved to Saipan about six weeks before I moved here. I had Googled Saipan and found Walt's blog. I left a comment that we should meet when I got there or something.
He never responded.

A few months later I ran into him at a Save the Grotto (http://savethegrotto.blogspot.com) meeting. We exchanged about 4 words and then he disappeared again.

It wasn't until 9 months after moving to Saipan that I finally had a real conversation with him…over the phone while he was back in New York. I won't get into the details, but two weeks later the We Love Saipan Network was born (www.welovesaipan.com).

Since then we have collaborated on building the Blogosphere on this island. We've inspired and coached people to create blogs. Some of the people we've coached are now coaching others. A year ago you could count the number of Saipan blogs on one hand. Now there are well over 100 and the bloggers meet up once a month for a blogger meetup.

This is an island where some of the managers who work for the government don't know how to use email. It was no small task in creating our blogger community and we both point to it as one of our big successes.

But you probably don't care too much about what Walt and I do on this rock in the Pacific. You bought this book because you want to join the ranks of people making money on the Internet. I am one of those people. I want to help you become one of those people, too.

Increasing Blog Traffic

Most, if not all, bloggers want to increase their blog traffic. I'm not going to pretend that I understand why, but I know that many bloggers, including me, track their blog stats religiously. We all want to know how many people are reading our blogs, where those people are, and how they are finding us. I do it and if you are reading this, I'm sure you do it too.

There are online programs out there which claim they will generate huge boosts of traffic to your blog. I've tried many of them. Most of them don't work as well as they promise. There are also websites out there promising to sell you their secret to creating tons of web traffic. I think most of them are scams. All the information they provide can be found for free somewhere else on the Internet, just maybe not all in the same place.

I have been blogging for three years and my personal website receives between 300-1000 unique visitors per day, with as many as 10,000 in a single day. I use a number of techniques and programs to keep that number growing. My goal is to become the most popular written media in my home of the Mariana Islands (Saipan is one of the 14 Mariana Islands). Right now that crown belongs to one of our local newspapers, which receives about 14,000 daily hits to their website.

I will make one disclaimer: The information I present in this chapter is all available online. Only problem is that it is spread throughout hundreds of websites, blogs and blog comments, and on discussion boards. I am not presenting anything new or earth shattering. The tools and techniques I present are all easy-to-use, pragmatic approaches to improving your Page Rank (PR), your Search Engine Optimization (SEO), and ultimately your website's traffic. With that said, let us begin.

Website Traffic generally comes from just a few sources.
a. Search engines
b. Links from other web pages
c. Email
d. Feeds
e. Browsers that have bookmarked your page or people who have memorized your unique URL

It is important to keep this in mind as you create your blog. You want to optimize your readership from all five sources.

Like I mentioned, it has taken three years of trial and error to come up with this stuff. If you want to save money, go right ahead and start plowing through the World Wide Web for this information, but if you want to save time, continue reading.

I have identified 10 easy steps to increase your Page Rank and improve the Search Engine Optimization of you blog.

201. ❏ Step 1: Create your blog ❏

The first thing a blogger needs to do in order to have a successful blog is to actually have a blog with content that is being updated on a regular basis. If you are going to attract readers, you have to have something for them to read. It should be regularly updated so that readers come back often to check for new content. Ideally it should be updated every single day; that way readers know to visit your blog daily.

When you start your blog, you want to choose a unique url and a blog title. For example, the url to my blog is http://jetapplicant.blogspot.com and the title is "The Saipan Blog – Saipan CNMI's most popular blog since ever since." You can change the title at any time, but the url will forever remain the same. I was applying for the JET program when I started my blog. I thought it was going to be a blog about applying for and then working for JET. Turned out it was going to be a blog about life in Saipan. Who knew?

202. ❏ Step 2: Update often ❏

Once you choose your url and your title and then start publishing, your website or blog will have a Page Rank of 0 and no other websites will link to it.

However, once you start updating regularly, after a few days readers will start to find your blog through search engines such as Google, Yahoo, and Technorati. If you create a blog using Blogger, it will appear in search results on Google Blogsearch seconds after you publish your first post. You'll have instant readership. If your website is interesting other webmasters who come across it will link to it, and then people will start visiting you via those links.

Most bloggers, though, prefer not to link to new blogs. Established bloggers like to link to other established blogs. Blogs start off and then go bust all the time. A blogger doesn't want to add a link to a blog that won't be around in a few months' time.

It will take time for your blog to make the switch from new blog to established blog, so just keep posting. It won't happen overnight, but it will happen. In the meantime, there are other ways to increase your readership.

203. ❏ Step 3: Add meta tags, labels, and ALT tags describing your blog ❏

Search Engine Optimization begins with the construction of your blog. Two ways to help search engines find your blog are to add meta tags to your template and to create a sitemap. Meta tags are simple. All you have to do is to come up with a list of keywords and a blog description that you think help explain your blog's content.

You are going to add two sets of meta data to your template.

The first one is a written description of your blog. It looks like this:

```
<meta content='Write up a description of your blog and put it here' name='Description'/>
```

Then you are going to create a list of keywords. It looks like this:

```
<meta content='create, a list, of keywords, that describe, your blog, and separate them, with commas' name='Keywords'/>
```

(a) Insert a description and keywords appropriate for your blog and copy and paste this code immediately after the <head> tag in your blog template. It is sometimes necessary to put a </meta> tag after this code.

Similar to meta tags are ALT tags on your photographs. If you use blogger to upload your photos, the html code for the photo will have some code that looks like ALT="". This allows you to label your pictures. Simply put your label between the two "" marks. For example, a photo George W. Bush playing golf could be labeled with ALT="George W. Bush playing golf". After your photo is published, when someone scrolls over the photo, the words "George W. Bush playing golf" will pop up. This tells your readers what the photo is and it helps search engines with image searches.

This works really well. My college friend, who uses the blogger moniker The Angry Sicilian, added a picture of an extinct woodpecker and labeled the ALT tag. He has been one of the top results of a google image search for this woodpecker for about two years now.

While we are on the topic of labels, it is also important to add labels to all of your posts describing what the post is about. Blogger makes this easy. There is a box on the bottom of the post form and you just fill in your labels, separated by commas. Other services may require you to write the html code for the labels.

Labels will help search engines, particularly blog search engines and directories find your blog. Want a quick cheat to generate a few instant hits? Go to www.technorati.com and see what the top 10 searches are for the day. Write a quick post about that topic, including the name in your title of the post, the body of the post, and the labels. Publish the post and ping Technorati. Technorati will crawl your blog and list you in the top of search results as the most recent post about said topic. You should get hits right away. I've done this and received a hundred hits in under an hour.

Creating and submitting a sitemap will also increase your SEO. This can be done through Google Webmaster Tools. Sign up at http://www.google.com/webmasters and follow the instructions. This online tool will also help you find any dead links on your webpage and will tell you the top searches people are using to find your blog, among many other things.

204. ❑ Step 4: Create a niche ❑

Depending on your blog's topic and the amount of other websites written about your topic, your blog will have either a high or a low position in search engine results for particular searches. You will appear somewhere on the results page within days, there is just no telling how high your rank will be. If your blog is a niche blog like The Saipan Blog, then your blog will appear very high in searches for "saipan." If your blog is about national politics or health care, it is going to have a hard time competing with established websites like CNN.com and WebMD.com in searches for things like "presidential election" or "health insurance." A niche blog is always better and is easier to optimize.

Now that your niche blog is well written, updated often, and uses meta tags, ALT tags, labels, and now that you've submitted a site map to Google, your SEO should be pretty good. Within a few days you should see your website rising dramatically in search engine results.

And when I say niche, the smaller the better. Create a compelling story, but make it specific. I am "the environmentalist party boy from Saipan with the hot Korean girlfriend." I am on the first page of almost every search that includes the word Saipan, whether it be Saipan Scuba, Saipan Tribune, Saipan Blog, or Saipan Pirates.

Even for the websites that charge a fee, almost everything ever written about boosting website traffic will claim that great content leads to lots of traffic. If only it were that easy. Great content will get people to come back to your blog; the difficult thing is getting new people to visit your blog in the first place.

In order to grow your blog readership, your PR ranking, and your search engine ranking you have to be constantly trying to attract new readers, especially new readers interested in your content. Those readers are more likely to be return visitors.

Last November, less than a year ago, I was desperately trying to get my blog traffic over 100 visitors per day. I'd have a good day every once in a while and jump to over 150 visits, but there were days when my traffic was as low as 50. I was averaging about 80.

Nine months later I am averaging between 300-500 unique visitors per day and I've had as many as 10,000 hits in one day. While this isn't the huge boost in traffic promised by the people selling huge boosts in traffic, it is a significant increase.

In nine months I've added, well, nine months worth of content, proper nouns, labels, and labeled photos to my blog,. There has been almost no change in my blogging formula. Except for a few changes, the template is pretty much exactly the same as it was two and a half years ago, I haven't bought a new camera, so I'm not posting better pictures. I certainly haven't gotten any funnier or any smarter, either.

What I have done over the last several months was to attract a large number of readers that have an interest in what I write. My blog, The Saipan Blog, is a niche blog. There aren't too many blogs, or even websites for that matter, about Saipan. Saipan is a small island in the Western Pacific with about 60,000 inhabitants. The Saipan Blog is a personal blog about my life, my work, my friends, and my little island home. While I'd like to think that the sky is the limit to my readership, there are a limited number of people in this world that would want to read something about Saipan, but I want to capture as many of them as I can.

205. ❏ Step 5: Use proper nouns ❏

When I was a kid, when I wanted to find information on something, I went to my local library, found the card catalog, and tried to decipher the Dewey Decimal system. These days I go to Google. Google can find almost anything I am looking for, so when I enter what I want to search for, I am as specific as possible.

That led me to discover a little trick that I use. I make my blog as specific as possible. If I go out to eat, I don't write about the Indian Restaurant Downtown. I write about Taste of India on the Paseo de Marianas in Garapan. I name the specific dishes. I throw in some ingredient names. I use lots of proper nouns. People tend to search for proper nouns when they use search engines, so filling your blog with them will greatly improve your SEO.

206. ❑ Step 6: Position yourself as an expert ❑

I write about life as an environmentalist living on a small island, my adventures exploring the island, meeting the people, and even my boring everyday activities. I throw in some politics, usually in an attempt to be funny, and I post photos and videos that I host on Youtube. That's pretty much it. My blog is nothing special. It is just a blog about life in Saipan.

Well, actually, it is not just a blog about life in Saipan. It is THE blog about life in Saipan. I chose "The Saipan Blog – Saipan, *CNMI's most popular blog since ever since" as my title. I could have called it anything. I could have called it "Angelo's Dumb Blog," "Adventures in Scuba Diving," "The Environmentalist Speaks." Those names describe what I write about, but they don't have the authority of The Saipan Blog. The name The Saipan Blog makes the reader think that this blog is the official or unofficial authority on everything having to do with Saipan. Adding further to my credibility as an expert on Saipan, I publish under the pen name, The Saipan Blogger.

Another great way to increase your credibility as an expert in your blogging niche is to constantly hyper link back to your earlier posts. This creates more internal links within your blog, gets the reader to dig through your archives, and makes you look more like an expert if this is something you have been talking about for a long time.

CNMI=Commonwealth of the Northern Mariana Islands, the official name of the 14 islands of which Saipan is the capital.

207. ❑ Step 7: Make a list of the potential readers you want to target ❑

If you were to stop reading this chapter right here, and only implement the previous 6 suggestions, eventually your blog would gain a strong following, it just might take a matter of months or years. This is something that you'll have to be creative with, but if you are to this point, I'm assuming that you have a clean, uncluttered template, that your content is interesting and descriptive enough that your use of proper nouns ensures that you pop up relatively high on search engine results and that you are using meta tags, labels and ALT tags.

The next step is to find more people and to get them to visit your blog one time. We'll worry about tools to get them to stay and then come back later, but first we need to find these potential readers.

Blogging is all about connecting with other people. I think most people post to blogs with the intention of having other people read what they have posted. Effective bloggers are effective communicators. You want to find potential readers and drive them to your blog.

When looking for traffic, it is important to target people who are very likely to have an interest in the topics you choose to write about. A list of categories of people that I think would have an interest in something called The Saipan Blog might include:

a. People I know, including friends, family, business associates, and other acquaintances
b. People from Saipan, either living here or living off island
c. People thinking of relocating to or visiting Saipan for a vacation
d. People interested in environmental issues, especially issues related to coral reefs and community organizing
e. People who have similar interests as me, such as divers, soccer players, amateur photographers
f. Democrats, especially Democrats interested in the Jack Abramoff and Tom Delay scandals
g. People applying to, or currently on the JET (Japan Exchange Teacher) program
h. Americans living abroad

So, ask yourself: Who are the potential readers for YOUR blog?

208. ❑ Step 8: Advertise your blog for free ❑

You want to target people who have an ongoing interest in your website so that they continue to revisit it often. If you target people not interested in your subject, they will visit once and not return.

NOTE: Do not SPAM people asking them to visit your blog or link to you.

There are a thousand ways to promote your blog for free. Simple things you can do to promote your blog are to:

(a) Add a line in your email signature telling people to visit your blog

(b) Put your website on your business card

(c) Wear a T-shirt with your url printed on it

(d) Add a line to your signature in online forums telling people about your blog

(e) Add your blog to blog directories. I like blogtopsites and blogtoplist, but there are dozens of these out there. Do a google search for "blog directory" to find the top ones. Don't forget to add the blog directory's button to your blog in a pleasant way. Too many is ugly. A lot of blog directories will republish your RSS feed, simultaneously creating new links and directing traffic to your blog.

(f) Register with Technorati. Add a Fave This Blog button to your blog.

(g) Add a link to your blog from your Myspace, Facebook, Twitter, and in the description of all of your Youtube and Google Video videos.

(h) When you upload videos to Youtube and Google Video, overlay the video with the url to your blog. Microsoft users can use Microsoft Movie Maker to edit the video. Apple has similar programs that are very easy to use.

(i) If you post pictures to your blog, edit each picture so that it contains your url and blog name

(j) Create buttons or banners for other blogs to use to link to you. I have done this with We Love Saipan and Beautify CNMI.

(k) Find websites that list websites in your town or state or about your topic and have your blog listed. For example, I am listed on sites about ex-pats, Saipan, and the JET Program

Getting people to link to you.
       If you have a great blog, people will just start linking to you. Really! The internet is like that! Get involved in the blogger community. After you have had a few back and forths in the comments section with another blogger, it is appropriate to ask them to exchange links. Spamming is never acceptable.

209. ❑ Step 9: Use free online services to improve the blogger experience ❑

Services that you must join/use are
(a) Technorati – register all of your blogs and add a "Fave this Blog" button to your blog
(b) Feedburner – this "burns" your feed. They offer many services. Make sure you add a "Subscribe" button to your blog
(c) Cafépress – Create an online store for your blog. You may never sell anything, but at least you'll have merchandise. Make sure all merchandise includes your url.
(d) Google Webmaster – will tell you how people are finding your blog. It will also help you create and upload a sitemap.
(e) Sitemeter- I like this counter
(f) Extreme Tracker- I like this counter, too. Each counter tracks different things.

210. ❑ Step 10: Get people to stay for a long time and return to your blog ❑

One of the worst things you could do is create a website with a high page rank that people easily find using search engines but where they spend only a few seconds before navigating to another page. You have to create a website that people stay on for a long time...and then come back to visit often.

A great way to get links is to link to yourself. You are already a niche blogger. Separate your different niches into separate blogs. If you have links in your sidebar, have them linked to your blog or to other blogs you publish. Put all your links in one place, preferably on a page other than the homepage.

The best way to get links is to link to others. Follow this formula: Find another blogger who wrote something you like. Write a post about it on YOUR blog. Leave a comment on that blogger's blog, telling them about the response. Chances are they will write a response to your blog on their blog, linking to your response. If they don't do this in a few days, leave another comment. Wait for their reply and then it is appropriate to discuss exchanging links.

Link to other blogs in the body of your posts, not in your sidebar. Too many links makes your blog look cluttered and unsightly. They also give readers the opportunity to navigate away from your page.

Start a blogger meetup in your area or join one that already exists.

Once you are doing all these things your Page Ranking should start going up. My blog is a PR4. Some blogs are as high as a PR7.

The algorithm Google uses to determine page rank is very complicated and always changing. They have hundreds of mathematicians working to constantly improve it. Google wants to tweak their algorithm so when a user needs to find information on a topic, they are directed to the best website with the best information on that topic.

Some of the things this algorithm takes into account are the number of other web pages linking to the site, the number of internal links, the lack of dead links, the content, the URL, title, meta tags, the level of traffic and visitor depth, the number of people clicking on the page when it pops up in a search result. I have even heard that they can check Gmail for the number of times a website link is emailed.

Finally, you want people to come back to your blog. This starts as early as deciding on your unique url. The blogger URL for one of my blogs is http://beautifycnmi.blogspot.com. That isn't very easy to remember, so I purchased www.beautifycnmi.com and I have it redirect to the blog. It only costs me $9 per year, but it makes it much easier for people to remember the URL.

Summary
1.   Create your blog
2.   Update often
3.   Add meta tags, labels, and ALT tags describing your blog
4.   Create a niche

5.   Use proper nouns
6.   Position yourself as an expert
7.   Make a list of the potential readers you want to target
8.   Advertise your blog for free
9.   Use free online services to improve the blogger experience
10.   Get people to stay for a long time and then come back to your blog

But, wait! There's more!
Other things you can do that I haven't:

211. ❑ You can pay for links. ❑

Yahoo and Google will advertise your blog for about $0.10 - $100.00 per click, depending on the keywords you want to advertise with. Those are pay per click programs. There are also more traditional, static ads where you pay a webmaster to link to you or show your banner on their page for a predetermined amount of time for a set cost. There is no guarantee of generating traffic and these programs can be expensive, but a link from a website with a high Page Rank can help increase your Page Rank in turn. It could have the side effect of increasing your rank in search engine results, so maybe it is worth it.

212. ❑ Read about Katie Rees and Technorati ❑

To finish this chapter, let me return to how I managed to top 90,600,000 other websites to become the number one search engine result for "Most Popular Blog Ever." Basically, my blog's PR4 combined with the full title of my blog, which is "The Saipan Blog – Saipan, CNMI's most popular blog since ever since" and the lack of other blogs including "most popular blog" in their titles put me there. There are plenty of websites that include "most popular blog" in their content, but I think there are very few that have that specific text in their titles. I'm sure that if a website with a higher PR were to put that in their title I would get bumped, so I hope no one thinks to do that. Chances are someone already has. I will be amazed that if by the time you read this I am still the #1 result.

If you have found this information useful, I hope that you will write a review of this book and my chapter in your blog. Please leave me a comment on my blog at http://www.thesaipanblogger.com letting me know what you thought. If you write a review and link to my blog, I will reciprocate with a link to your blog in one of my blog posts.

213. ❑ See Problogger.net for tips on generating income ❑

[END OF ANGELO'S BONUS CHAPTER]

MY NOT-SO-SECRET BUSINESS MODELS, PRODUCT IDEAS & SALES STRATEGIES

"Here are some business models that work for me and others."

214. ❏ Use my book selling strategy ❏

The strategy:

(a) I create info products and biographies and other guides and manuals

(b) I create a separate website for each product in order to focus online search.

(c) I treat each new product as being the first of a new category/niche.

(d) I sell the ebooks and paperbacks directly through my site,

(e) The ebooks are immediately downloaded through x-cart, and the paperbacks are printed and shipped by Createspace

215. ❏ Use my Amazon strategy ❏

I consider the sales I make on Amazon as part of my websites that sell strategy. Amazon has a great brand identity in the minds of the consumer. Customers will often land on my site first, then go to Amazon to make their purchase. It makes sense, therefore, not to view Amazon as a competitor, but as an ally with a powerful brand identity and customer base.

The strategy:

(a) Include your affiliate account links from your site to your product page on Amazon's site. I am also an Amazon Associate/Affiliate. If you look on my sites you'll see an option for people to purchase my books through Amazon. I usually place my associate code in this link so that if they do, and/or if they purchase ANYTHING from Amazon, I earn a commission. (Not a big money maker for me, but I know bloggers who do quite well with this strategy)

(b) Register with Amazon Marketplace. I place my own listing in the Amazon Marketplace. If you look to the right of the regular listing, you'll see people selling used copies of the book listed. I offer an autographed copy at a price just a few pennies less than the regular listing. I make more money per sale through this method, but there aren't as many takers. When orders come in, I ship this out myself via Media Mail.

216. ❏ Become a tour guide?? ❏

The strategy:

(a) visit exotic lands

(b) make friends with local vendors

(c) provide them customers as a middle man or conduct tours yourself!

This is part of my nomadpreneur strategy! Learn more in the Nomadpreneur SECRETS manual. Visit: http://www.discoversaipan.com

217. ❑ Re-issue public domain work ❑

The strategy:

(a) find a public domain book

(b) re-issue it

(c) market it better than the original!

http://www.fastandgrowyoung.com

218. ❑ Start and grow a community ❑

While I don't personally maintain a bulletin board for a community, my online buddy, Winston Wu of HappierAbroad.com does, is very good at it, and uses phpbb.

http://www.happierabroad.com

http://www.phpbb.com

219. ❑ Set up a subscription product ❑

One of the best types of income to generate is subscription income. It's passive, it's recurring. Your Paypal account has a feature whereby your subscribers' credit cards can be billed automatically each month, week, or at whatever interval you decide. The ideal scenario is to offer a subscription to a newsletter, or set up recurring billing for advertising space on your site.

Check out the "Steel Pipe" Newsletter at http://www.fittobreed.com

220. ❑ Consider my joint venture strategy ❑

Strategy: Pursue joint ventures with sites that already have traffic

A few years ago, the owner of the now-defunct getsigned.com contacted me for us to work together. He liked my products, and because of his own expertise and positioning had more traffic to his sites than I did. We worked together, and it was one of the best business decisions I made. His traffic, combined with my unique products

221. ❑ Sell t-shirts and merchandise ❑

http://www.cafepress/freesummer

222. ❏ Consider the donation/contribution model ❏

The Strategy: Give it away free, and request donations

How it works

Beginning in 1995, and every summer since, I've compiled all the free concerts happening in New York City and offer the listings free of charge on my http://www.FreeSummerConcerts.com site. The listings are "unveiled" a month at a time. So, for example, you can't access the July calendar of events until the last week in June. However, the impatient New York resident/tourist can become a VIP by "donating" $10 or more and thereby receive ALL the summer's events in advance! That's it!

What happens

The majority of people on my list of over 10,000 simply wait for my weekly emails to be updated about the week's events. However, quite a few donate the $10 to become VIPs. Some donate $5. And I've even gotten dollar bills sent by regular mail to my PO box! But, here's the cool part. Many people donate much more than the minimum! Some donate $20. Some donate $50.

The largest single donation so far has been $200! People start searching for summer events as early as January 1! I fully expect that I'll soon start receiving donations for the 2014 season in a few days but don't need to start compiling the events until mid-to-late Spring.

Why it works

- My lists are thorough and accurate
- I add a personal touch (commentary, suggestions) to the emails I send out
- Yes, all the information is readily available on individual event/promoter sites, but people don't mind paying to have all the listings in one place rather than having to do the compilations themselves
- The concept of being a "donor" appeals to a certain segment of the population--a segment that sometimes has cash to spare.
- I'm a nice guy with positive expectations

Caveats:

- this is ONE strategy of many that can create multiple small-but-cumulative streams of income
- there are, of course, other factors why this may/may NOT work for you: your personality, expectations, credibility, track record, level of professionalism, site design, product, timeliness, geography
- It's "seasonally passive" in that I do the compilation once each year over the course of few weeks, and then everything runs on automatic. I spent hundreds of hours last year creating software to automate as much of the process as possible, and to allow for others to input events and even manage listings for their region.

NOTE: For the first few years, the site was completely free--just offered by me as a labor of passion--while my list of subscribers grew. One summer, however, I got up one day and just had the idea to place a donate button on the site. Within two hours, I got my first donation!....and then tweaked the strategy to what it is today!

BOTTOM LINE: Place a "donate" button on your existing site. You might be surprised what happens!

SECTION: OTHER STREAMS OF INCOME
"Here are other ways to offer value and generate income through your website!"

ADVERTSING INCOME

223. ❑ Set up a Google Adsense™ account ❑

Adsense is an income earning program for websites. The website owner gives Google website space for Google's ads to appear. Payment to the website owners is based on actual ad clicks. Ads are often similar to topics that appear on the website owner's site.
https://www.google.com/adsense

224. ❑ Set up a Textlinkbrokers account ❑

Your site may not qualify at this time if your site is brand new, but over time, due to the number of visitors to your site, and/or your site's PageRank, you can earn a fair amount of passive income by selling text links on your site. Here's how it works: If your site has achieved a PageRank of, say, 3 or more, there will be other site owners of lesser pageranked sites who will pay to have a link to their site appear on your site to help boost their PageRank. A site link Textlinkbrokers.com, as the name implies, acts as a broker between you and those sites looking for you!
http://www.textlinkbrokers.com

225. ❑ Set up Linkworth account ❑

Linkworth is also a broker of text links. I've used them with great success.
http://www.linkworth.com

226. ❑ Set up an affiliate program ❑

Setting up an affiliate program will result in many websites linking to you, which will positively affect your ranking in the search engines.

SECTION: OTHER SALES CHANNELS
"Here are other places your products can sell!"

227. ❑ Sell your product on eBay ❑
http://www.ebay.com

228. ❑ Sell your services through elance ❑
http//www.elance.com

229. ❑ Build your seller reputation on Amazon first ❑
If you start out as an Amazon vendor, you can then transition to being an independent online vendor. Include a business card with your standalone website and a discount code (for 10%, for example) to encourage your Amazon customers to order directly from your website.

SECTION: ONGOING & DAILY ACTIVITIES

"These are the things I (and other webmasters) do on a regular basis that keep the websites selling and the money coming in:"

Communicate - the more you communicate, the more money you earn.
Interact - find a way for your visitors to interact with you
Automate - the more you automate your system, the freer you become

230. ❑ Work from lists ❑

"All great achievers work from lists."-- **Brian Tracy**, *The Psychology of Achievement*

With 20 books and thirty websites to my credit, there are always new ideas and things to do popping into my head. Whenever a new idea or task comes to mind, I stop what I'm doing and add it to the appropriate list. I've got a computer file called ongoinglists.txt that's always open on my desktop while I work. It includes ongoing lists of "sites to update," "people to contact," "books to edit," "new titles," new business/product ideas to start" and more. Training myself to always create or add to a list before engaging in a new project or task accomplishes the following:

(a) prevents me from being distracted and jumping to do the immediate thing

(b) frees my mind to return to the task at hand knowing I won't forget

(c) creates a task list for myself or anyone else I may hire; there's always something to do

(d) documents a step-by-step process I can implement for future projects

Every random thought, no matter how seemingly trivial, has power and potential to develop into something more. The trick is to recognize, respect and honor the still small voice of success that often speaks to you in this way.
Tip: As you review your list, ask yourself "Can I do this NOW?" "What would happen if I announced the website now instead of after I design it?" Get in the habit of pushing yourself forward in this way. It takes courage.

231. ❑ Communicate with your mailing list ❑

Every time I communicate with my list, I make a few sales!

232. ❏ Review the sales process ❏

Every so often, pretend you are a new visitor and review the sales process to make sure all links are working, all instructions are clear, and that an actual order can be successfully completed and downloaded. Send an email to yourself to make sure all communication channels are working correctly. Tweak as necessary.

233. ❏ Follow up with customers ❏

Don't forget about your customers once they've purchased from you. Even if you have no additional products to sell them, make a point to send an occasional email asking them how they are enjoying their purchase.

234. ❏ Continue adding testimonials to your site ❏

This is a never-ending process. It doesn't matter how successful your product becomes, you should treat each person's feedback as if you're hearing it for the first time! Get their testimonial and feature it on a page on your site!

235. ❏ Continue testing different headlines and layouts ❏

236. ❏ Send link exchange letters to other webmasters ❏

237. ❏ Post comments on other sites and blogs ❏

238. ❏ Set up Google Alerts to monitor your industry ❏

A Google "alert" is a way to monitor the internet. The Google.com search engine provides a feature and service whereby you can receive an email notice any time a website or blog posts a story or release containing a specific keyword.

For example, let's say you have a business that relates to dog grooming. You set up a Google alert for the key word "dog grooming" and whenever a forum discussion, blog post, personal or business website, eBay listing, Amazon product etc appears on the internet with the words "dog grooming" a notice with a synopsis of the post along with an extract of how paragraph/sentence in which the key word appears is created and sent to you.

You can then decide if this is a relevant post for you to follow up with. If it's a forum discussion, you can join in and mention your product/service (be careful, as forums and bulletin boards have rules about blatant advertising of your product/service). If it's a blog post, you can leave a comment. The alert may mention events, people, organizations that are important for you to add to your communication lines, contact, offer review copies or suggest a sale.

You can set up your alerts to be sent to your inbox "as they happen" or once a day or once a week.

This is a great way for you to monitor your industry and gives you continuous marketing "to do" list to work on your Penny Power Marketing Campaign. Every little bit helps!

239. ❏ Submit articles to article distribution sites ❏

240. ❏ Send "available for interview" email to media ❏

241. ❏ Send a regular newsletter to your mailing list ❏

242. ❏ Ask influential people and customers to post reviews of your product on sites like Amazon.com where you have your products ❏

243. ❏ Post regularly to Facebook or Twitter ❏

244. ❏ Visit webmasterworld.com. Learn what other webmasters are doing ❏

245. ❏ Post daily to your blog ❏

246. ❏ Solicit product reviews from customers ❏

247. ❏ Work with HARO ❏

248. ❑ Distribute press release(s) ❑

249. ❑ Comment on LinkedIn groups ❑

250. ❑ Conduct events, teleclasses, discussion groups ❑

251. ❑ Create new products and update existing ones ❑

SECTION: MY EXPENSES

"Here's what it might cost you to maintain a basic website that sells, using Paypal as your credit card processor, a paid option for a shopping cart, and if you designed the site yourself."

252. ❑ Check out my expenses ❑

One-time costs:

      X-cart shopping cart $195.00 (X-cart Gold; Classic)

Monthly Costs:

      Paypal Payments Pro: $30.00/month + transaction fees

Annual Costs:

      Hosting account (1and1.) $71.99 ($5.99/month payable in advance)
      Register domain (powerpipe) $13.10/year
      SSL Certificate $49.00/year

Optional:

      Physical PO Box: $120.00/year US mainland;
      efax: $ 4.95/month

Free:

      Google Voice: $ 0.00
      Skype: $ 0.00
      Freeconferencecall.com $ 0.00

NOT INCLUDED: Appropriate business license/renewal fees, website design, logo design, image purchase, manufacturing costs.

For even more insights into how I incorporate these and other tools into my nomadpreneur lifestyle, check out Nomadpreneur SECRETS manual!

SECTION: GROWING GLOBAL
"The world awaits!

253. ❑ Recognize and respond to increasing demand ❑
Is your site ready to handle the big time? Is your manufacturing and distribution channel prepared for the large orders? Plan for:
how to fill 50 orders per day
how to to handle 1000 visits per hour to your site

254. ❑ Think in bigger chunks ❑
Rather than thinking of selling 1 product to 100 customers, think in terms of selling 100 units of that product to a single customer. Sell to:
Chain store buyers
MLM distributors
The military, etc.

255. ❑ Think in terms of countries instead of customers ❑
In an increasingly global economy, you must see your potential market in terms of multiple countries rather than simply states or counties in your home country.

256. ❑ Charge more ❑
It seems almost laughably obvious, but the best way to recession-proof your business is to raise your prices, sell to the people with money—those who are affected least and last by the recession—and REFUSE to compete with others on price, but to compete on uniqueness and value in order to justify your prices. Dan Kennedy shows you how.

257. ❑ Create a constant stream of prospects ❑
One of the ways I've created a constant stream of prospects for my tour guide business is to have my site featured on a travel site (cruisecritic, usatoday, wikitravel, etc.) These resources provide a constant stream of potential customers.

258. ❑ Build it to flip it ❑
A few years ago, Entrepreneur® Magazine asked me to write an article in which I interviewed several million-dollar passionpreneurs and asked them the secret to success. Almost every single one of them credited what they learned in

Michael Gerber's The E-myth Revisited to helping them think differently about business in general and about their own businesses in particular and has made the single most significant impact in the results they achieved.

After reading that book myself, the concept that impacted me the most, that has lingered until now, and that admittedly has been the most difficult to embrace has been: "The only reason to start a business, is to sell it."

Ever since reading that book (twice now), I've structured my businesses and designed the software that runs my sites with an eye on making it all turnkey operation that could be sold to and operated by someone else. Everything is template-based (that's why I was able to reserve discoverpagan, launch it 24 hours later, and earned $10,000 gross sale through it all within 30 days!) I already have the operations manuals for everything I do! Next step: read it again so that I can kick things up a notch or three!

259. ❑ Read: The E-Myth Revisited: Why Most Small Businesses Don't Work and What to Do About It by Michael E. Gerber ❑

260. ❑ Create worldwide movements ❑

This is actually much easier than you may realize given the reach of the internet. By being sensitive to the cultural nuances, languages, regulations and worldviews of a global market, you can modify your website to welcome people from around the world. All it takes these days is a Twitter or Youtube account, the right message, and amazing things can happen!
Read: *Revolution 2.0: The Power of the People is Greater than the People in Power*

261. ❑ Enter a new genre or part of the industry ❑

Don't limit yourself to one area of expertise and focus. If you are into music production, consider the opportunities in distribution. If you are a singer, be open to opportunities in composing.

262. ❑ Diversify ❑

When I was learning how to type in high school, who would have predicted I would use that skill to write my first 200-page book in under four weeks? Who could have predicted that when I learned Fortran in college, that the concept of logic I learned would empower me tackle learning HTML years later when the internet came along? Who could have predicted that that basic comfort with programming and design would give me tools to create a website in a day, and earn a $10,000 sale in less than 30 days? This journey has been an evolution where every milestone has been built on the one before.

Everything I've learned by creating websites that sell and marketing them effectively have helped me increase my areas of expertise and my channels of income to now include the industries of publishing, design, tourism and even real estate! My advice to you: diversify!

RECAP OF ALL STEPS

"Here's everything we just covered! Print and post where you can see it!"

SECTION: A FEW RECENT TESTIMONIALS
- ❑ 1. Meet Mel
- ❑ 2. Meet Chief Ray
- ❑ 3. Meet Tim
- ❑ 4. Read more testimonials

SECTION: REGISTRATION AND SUGGESTED PRE-REQUISITES
- ❑ 5. Complete the course sign-in and registration
- ❑ 6. Listen to my coaching sessions or workshops
- ❑ 7. Listen to recordings of interviews
- ❑ 8. Read *Turn Your Passion Into Profit*
- ❑ 9. Read the *Quick Start Manual*

SECTION: THIS MANUAL
- ❑ 10. Understand the goal of this manual
- ❑ 11. Commit to using this manual effectively
- ❑ 12. Understand what this manual offers
- ❑ 13. Make note of and use the after-purchase support

SECTION: ORIENTATION
- ❑ 14. Understand how to achieve anything you desire
- ❑ 15. Understand the real reasons my websites sell

SECTION: INTERNET PRIMER
- ❑ 16. Prepare for the underlying challenge
- ❑ 17. Read: How I Made My First Million on the Internet and how you can too
- ❑ 18. Understand the ways your website may actually generate income for you
- ❑ 19. Read: *Webonomics: 9 essential principles for growing your business on the world wide web*

SECITON 1: YOUR IDENTITY
- ❑ 20. Take the PassionPreneur Personality Test™
- ❑ 21. Complete the PassionProfit Coaching Questionnaire
- ❑ 22. Read: *In Search of a Better Belief System*
- ❑ 23. Raise your belief level
- ❑ 24. Read: *Secrets of the Millionaire Mind* by T. Harv Ecker
- ❑ 25. Embrace selling...not "shamelessly," but with pride
- ❑ 26. Read: *The Science of Getting Rich* by Wallace Wattles

SECTION: YOUR BUSINESS IDENTITY
- ❏ 27. Focus on the consumer
- ❏ 28. Read: *How to Win Friends and Influence People* by Dale Carnegi
- ❏ 29. Envision your brand
- ❏ 30. Read and apply *The 22 Immutable Laws of Branding*
- ❏ 31. Review this Branding Questionnaire Sample
- ❏ 32. Complete the Branding Questionnaire for YOUR business
- ❏ 33. Design/Create your logo
- ❏ 34. Create a tag line

SECTION: THE BASICS
- ❏ 35. Prepare the basics of what you will need
- ❏ 36. Choose the "right" domain
- ❏ 37. Reserve blog name, facebook page, twitter account
- ❏ 38. Set up hosting account
- ❏ 39. Request an SSL Certificate
- ❏ 40. Set a date for your launch
- ❏ 41. Upload a "coming soon" home page
- ❏ 42. Set up your domain-specific email accounts
- ❏ 43. Set up Paypal account
- ❏ 44. Integrate a shopping cart

SECTION 1: YOUR PRODUCT
- ❏ 45. Memorize my favorite definition of a product
- ❏ 46. Choose the right product
- ❏ 47. Price your product effectively
- ❏ 48. Establish a manufacturing and fulfillment strategy
- ❏ 49. Read: "The Case for Createspace"
- ❏ 50. Prepare your product
- ❏ 51. Pre-sell your product/service
- ❏ 52. Plan for empire

SECTION: INSTALLATION AND CONFIGURATION
- ❏ 53. Review how long it might take to install X-cart

SECTION: WEBSITE LAYOUT/DESIGN
- ❏ 54. Develop your ability to recognize a good website
- ❏ 55. Search online for free website templates

FLOW AND ACTIONS
- ❏ 56. Include a navigation bar on top, side and bottom of site pages
- ❏ 57. Get people to the cart environment as quickly as possible
- ❏ 58. Ask for the desired action and make it clickable
- ❏ 59. Add "Join mailing list" or "subscribe"

❑ 60. Focus on only one or two actions per page
❑ 61. Add a "tell a friend" form/link
❑ 62. Include social network buttons
❑ 63. Add a survey
❑ 64. Add a donate button
❑ 65. Add a popup that evades popup blockers
❑ 66. Add a "return to site" link to every landing page

LAYOUT AND DESIGN
❑ 67. Make the site "responsive"
❑ 68. Use long-form webpage format
❑ 69. Fit everything into the top screen "above the fold"
❑ 70. Focus on fewer products per site

IMAGES & VIDEO
❑ 71. Invest in professional, high quality images
❑ 72. Choose the best image format
❑ 73. Watermark all your images
❑ 74. Use a 3-Dimensional image
❑ 75. Design your banner and icons
❑ 76. Use video if appropriate

LINKS
❑ 77. Eliminate extraneous outbound links
❑ 78. Incorporate adequate free space
❑ 79. Place a phone number in your title tag

LANGUAGE TO INCLUDE
❑ 80. Lead with customer testimonials
❑ 81. Include third party, industry endorsements
❑ 82. Include "in business since"
❑ 83. Include the VISA/MC/AMEX/DISCOVER logos
❑ 84. Offer Paypal as a payment option
❑ 85. Offer customers options/variations/versions of product
❑ 86. Mention "secure server" on the order form
❑ 87. Include a privacy statement
❑ 88. Add (and honor) a 100% money-back guarantee
❑ 89. Don't forget international customers
❑ 90. Add telephone number prominently on site
❑ 91. Mention "bulk sales" if applicable

TOOLS
❑ 92. Add a tracker code

ADVANCED FEATURES, BELLS AND WHISTLES

- ❑ 93. Enjoy this inspiring story
- ❑ 94. Checkout the geopopup script
- ❑ 95. Add a time/date stamp or countdown
- ❑ 96. Add a clickable map of the US or world
- ❑ 97. Allow public to upload their images
- ❑ 98. Customizable Facebook "Like" box
- ❑ 99. On-click select all
- ❑ 100. Texting with Paypal
- ❑ 101. Send money via mobile phone
- ❑ 102. Show Twitter followers as text
- ❑ 103. Show Facebook followers as text
- ❑ 104. A simple drop down menu
- ❑ 105. Collapsible text
- ❑ 106. An external feed

SECTION: SEARCH ENGINE OPTIMIZATION (SEO)

- ❑ 107. Read article on Google Page Rank
- ❑ 108. Make a keyword list
- ❑ 109. Add keywords to keyword meta tag
- ❑ 110. Add keywords to description meta tag
- ❑ 111. Add keywords to image "alt" and "title" tags
- ❑ 112. Become a webmaster that sells!

SECTION: YOUR WEBSITE SALES COPY

- ❑ 113. Use second person voice
- ❑ 114. Create a winning headline
- ❑ 115. Collect testimonials
- ❑ 116. Visualize your ideal prospect/customer
- ❑ 117. Relate to your prospect
- ❑ 118. Understand what motivation moves people to action
- ❑ 119. Use the following words in your sales copy
- ❑ 120. Use keywords in your sales copy
- ❑ 121. Use "fear of loss" and a sense of urgency
- ❑ 122. Use the "Web Copy Template" to create your compelling sales pitch
- ❑ 123. Add something timely and relevant
- ❑ 124. Write a short version and long version of product description
- ❑ 125. Write short version and long version of author/bio/founder bio
- ❑ 126. Use everything above to create your press release at the same time
- ❑ 127. Make sure spelling is correct

SECTION: INITIAL LAUNCH AND TESTING

- ❑ 128. Upload your site
- ❑ 129. Test for HTML compliance
- ❑ 130. Test all links
- ❑ 131. Test how your site appears on multiple devices

SECTION: TESTING AND SPEED IMPROVEMENTS

- ❑ 132. Test your site for speed
- ❑ 133. Add compression code above header
- ❑ 134. Test if your Gzip code is working
- ❑ 135. Remove unused CSS code
- ❑ 136. Minify/compress Javascript, CSS and HTML
- ❑ 137. Test if your site's compression code is working
- ❑ 138. Defer Javascript (Place Javascript at bottom)
- ❑ 139. Optimize images
- ❑ 140. Use an appropriate image file format
- ❑ 141. Specify exact image dimensions
- ❑ 142. Serve scaled images
- ❑ 143. Place css code inline
- ❑ 144. Reduce external references
- ❑ 145. Test in different browsers
- ❑ 146. Look at my speed test results and improvements
- ❑ 147. Seek out support

SECTION: BECOME A WEBMASTER THAT SELLS

- ❑ 148. Join and participate at WebmasterWorld.com
- ❑ 149. Visit, browse and join Problogger.net mailing list
- ❑ 150. Start a Google Webmaster Tools Account
- ❑ 151. Start Bing Webmaster Account
- ❑ 152. Set up a Google Analytics account

SECTION: MARKETING, PROMOTION & PUBLICITY

- ❑ 153. Understand and implement Non-existence Formula
- ❑ 154. Find lines of communication
- ❑ 155. Make yourself known
- ❑ 156. Discover out what is needed or wanted
- ❑ 157. Produce or deliver it
- ❑ 158. Create sitemap
- ❑ 159. Write press releases
- ❑ 160. Write articles

FREE OPTIONS
❑ 161. Register your site with google.com
❑ 162. Submit URL and sitemap to search engines
❑ 163. Announce to mailing lists
❑ 164. Submit press releases
❑ 165. Submit articles
❑ 166. Finance/publicize your project on kickstarter, et.al

BECOME AN EXPERT AND COMMENTATOR
❑ 167. Become a HARO expert
❑ 168. Do guest blog posts
❑ 169. Request reviews on Amazon, et.al
❑ 170. Request reviews and links from related sites
❑ 171. Answer questions on expert sites
❑ 172. Post to bulletin boards
❑ 173. Comment on articles in your field
❑ 174. Add to wikipedia, wikitravel, et.al

COMMUNITY BUZZ BUILDING
❑ 175. Start and grow a mailing list of email subscribers
❑ 176. Start and grow a forum community
❑ 177. Start and build a Twitter following
❑ 178. Start and grow a Facebook group
❑ 179. Set up a Youtube channel
❑ 180. Keep up with the latest social networks

OTHER BUZZ BUILDING STRATEGIES
❑ 181. Add a signature file to your outgoing emails
❑ 182. Create a short kindle ebook
❑ 183. Read what works for me

A FEW PAID STRATEGIES (ADVERTISING)
❑ 184. Use Google's Adwords Program
❑ 185. Place classified ads in college newspapers

SECTION: PRICING STRATEGY
❑ 186. Resolve to NEVER compete on price!
❑ 187. Read: No B.S. Marketing to the Affluent by Dan Kennedy

SECTION: SALES STRATEGIES

❑ 188. Read what works for me for generating LINEAR, RESIDUAL income
❑ 189. Read what works for me for generating PASSIVE income
❑ 190. Read what works for me for generating CONTRIBUTION income

SECTION: MONITORING YOUR SITE

❑ 191. Track visits to your website
❑ 192. Track clicks to your shopping cart and checkout
❑ 193. Proceed, adjust course, rinse & repeat!

SECTION: YOUR MAILING LIST

❑ 194. Set up a list management system
❑ 195. Set up an auto-responder system
❑ 196. Implement the "Bulk Senders Guidelines"
❑ 197. Include a link to your product/site in all outgoing emails
❑ 198. Communicate regularly with your followings (Facebook, Twitter, et.al.)
❑ 199. Communicate regularly with your email list
❑ 200. Blog regularly

SECTION: ANGELO'S BONUS CHAPTER

❑ 201. Create your blog
❑ 202. Update often
❑ 203. Add meta tags, labels and ALT tags
❑ 204. Create a niche
❑ 205. Use proper nouns
❑ 206. Position yourself as an expert
❑ 207. Make a list of potential readers
❑ 208. Advertise your blog for free
❑ 209. Use free online services to improve the blogger experience
❑ 210. Get people to stay for a long time and then come back to your blog
❑ 211. Pay for links
❑ 212. Read about Katie Rees and Technorati
❑ 213. See Problogger.net for advice

SECTION: MY NOT-SO-SECRET BUSINESS MODELS, PRODUCT IDEAS & SALES STRATEGIES

❑ 214. Use my book selling strategy
❑ 215. Use my Amazon strategy
❑ 216. Become a tour guide??
❑ 217. Reissue public domain work
❑ 218. Start and grow a community

❑ 219. Create a subscription product
❑ 220. Consider my joint venture strategy
❑ 221. Sell t-shirts and other merchandise
❑ 222. Consider the donation/contribution model

SECTION: OTHER STREAMS OF INCOME
❑ 223. Set up a Google Adsense™ account
❑ 224. Set up a Textlinkbrokers account
❑ 225. Set up a Linkworth account
❑ 226. Set up an affiliate program

SECTION: OTHER SALES CHANNELS
❑ 227. Sell your product on eBay.com
❑ 228. Sell your services through Elance.com
❑ 229. Build your seller reputation on Amazon first

SECTION: ONGOING & DAILY ACTIVITIES
❑ 230. Work from lists
❑ 231. Communicate with your mailing list
❑ 232. Review the sales process
❑ 233. Follow up with customers
❑ 234. Continue adding testimonials to your site
❑ 235. Continue testing different headlines and layouts
❑ 236. Send out link exchange letters to other webmasters
❑ 237. Post comments on other blogs
❑ 238. Use Google alerts to keep abreast of your keywords
❑ 239. Submit articles to article distribution sites
❑ 240. Send announcement letter/release/available for interview to media
❑ 241. Send a regular newsletter to your mailing list
❑ 242. Ask others to post reviews of your product on sites like Amazon.com
❑ 243. Post regularly to Facebook or Twitter
❑ 244. Visit webmasterworld.com to learn what other webmasters are doing
❑ 245. Post daily to your blog
❑ 246. Solicit product reviews/testimonials from customers
❑ 247. Work with HARO
❑ 248. Distribute press releases
❑ 249. Comment on LinkedIn Groups
❑ 250. Conduct Events, Teleclasses, discussion groups
❑ 251. Create new products and update existing ones

SECTION: MY EXPENSES

❑ 252. Check out my expenses

SECTION: GROWING GLOBAL

❑ 253. Recognize and respond to increasing demand.

❑ 254. Think in bigger chunks.

❑ 255. Think in terms of countries instead of customers.

❑ 256. Charge more.

❑ 257. Create a constant stream of prospects.

❑ 258. Build it to flip it

❑ 259. Read: *The E-myth Revisited*

❑ 260. Create worldwide movements.

❑ 261. Enter a new genre or part of the industry

❑ 262. Diversify!

Note: at any given time, I may be tweaking some of these strategies on my own websites in order to improve them. Consequently, you may, for instance visit a site and NOT see a particular item that has been suggested. Not to worry. The suggestions in this manual have all worked for me and others.

RECAP OF ALL LINKS IN THIS MANUAL
(in order of appearance)

[This information is current, and all the links work as of May 2014. After 6 months (i.e. after Oct 2014), check http://www.passionprofit.com/wts/resources/ for any updates.]

*items with an asterisk are recommendations that may change. Visit http://www.passionprofit.com/wts for the latest recommendations

http://www.passionprofit.com/wts/contribute
http://www.globaltindahan.com
http://www.civilianside.com
http://www.passionprofit.com/testimonials
http://www.passionprofit.com/store/product.php?productid=20 | (6-CD audio)
http://www.waltgoodridge.com/interviews | (Listen to my interviews)
http://www.passionprofit.com/store/product.php?productid=1 (Passion ebook)
http://www.passionprofit.com/store/product.php?productid=26 (Quickstart)
http://www.passionprofit.com/wts (Websites That Sell Resources home page)
http://www.passionprofit.com/store/product.php?productid=19 (Websites-Sell paper)

SECTION: YOUR IDENTITY
http://www.passionprofit.com/itest (Take the Passionpreneur Personality Test)
http://www.passionprofit.com/wts/coaching (View the Coaching Questionnaire)
http://www.passionprofit.com/free (In Search of a Better Belief System free)
http://www.betterbeliefsystem.com (Better Belief System PAPERBACK)
http://www.kickstarter.com (a crowd funding site)

SECTION: YOUR BUSINESS IDENTITY
http://www.changethegamebook.com (branding questionnaire applied)

SECTION: THE BASICS
http://www.1and1.com (for hosting)*
http://www.passionprofit.com/wts/comingsoon (a sample "coming soon" page)
http://www.Paypal.com (for credit card processing)*
http://www.x-cart.com (for shopping cart)*
http://www.passionprofit.com/wts/paypalcarts.html (Paypal-supported carts)
http://www.fastandgrowyoung.com (my current top seller)
http://www.saipanfactorygirl.com (my previous top seller)
http://www.createspace.com (for product manufacturing)
http://www.saipanpreneur.com/archives/203/ (why Createspace is a good option)

SECTION: YOUR WEBSITE LAYOUT/DESIGN

http://www.whichtestwon.com (guess which site design is more effective)

http://www.designrazzi.com/2013/free-wordpress-themes/ (free templates)

http://www.1001freewpthemes.com/ (more free website templates)

http://www.addthis.com (provides code to add social network buttons)

http://www.passionprofit.com/wts/popup (see the evade browser popup in action)

http://www.123RF.com (for purchasing images at low cost)

http://www.alamy.com (for purchasing images)

http://kimbriggs.com/computers/computer-software/perl-image-manipulation.file (add watermark to images)

http://www.grsites.com/generate/generator/1/ (curved text logo generator)

http://www.1001FreeFonts.com

http://dabuttonfactory.com/

http://www.bestofsaipan.com (great array of (my) banners)

http://www.extremetracker.com (great free tracker)

http://www.javascriptsource.com (a lot of bells and whistles)

http://www.freesummerconcerts.com (my story of inspiration)

http://www.passionprofit.com/wts/geopopup (see the geopopup script in action)

http://www.freesummerconcerts.com (clickable map of US)

http://php.about.com/od/advancedphp/ss/php_file_upload.htm (upload images)

http://www.mybloggertricks.com/2011/06/customize-facebook-like-box-with-css.html (customizable facebook like box)

http://stackoverflow.com/questions/1173194/select-all-div-text-with-single-mouse-click (On-click Select All)

https://www.paypal.com/us/webapps/mpp/mobile/mobile-text (Texting Paypal)

https://www.paypal.com/us/webapps/helpcenter/article/?articleID=94016&m=SRE (Send Money via mobile phone)

http://www.bloggertricksandtoolz.com/2011/02/how-to-show-display-number-of-twitter.html (Display the number of Twitter followers as text

http://www.bloggertipandtrick.net/2010/05/display-twitter-follower-number-as-text.html (Display the number of Twitter followers as text

https://gist.github.com/599243 (Display Facebook followers as text)

http://javascriptsource.com/navigation/simple-drop-down-menu.html (drop down)

http://www.sivamdesign.com/scripts/dwld/col_text.html (collapsible text)

http://www.saipanliving.com/immigration.html (external feed; iframe)

SECTION: SEARCH ENGINE OPTIMIZATION

http://www.webworkshop.net/pagerank.htm (Article on Google Pagerank)

https://adwords.google.com/select/KeywordToolExternal (Keyword tool)

http://www.keywordspy.com (Keyword selection tool)

http://www.keywordeye.co.uk (Keyword selection tool)

http://www.semrush.com (Keyword selection tool)

http://www.googlekeywordtool.com/ (keyword optimization)

SECTION: YOUR WEBSITE SALES COPY
http://www.passionprofit.com/wts/300bestheadlines (idea-generating headlines)

SECTION: INITIAL LAUNCH & TESTING
http://validator.w3.org (test your HTML code for compliance)
http://www.iphonetester.com/ (test on various mobile devices)
http://www.mobilephoneemulator.com/ (test on various mobile devices)
http://ipadpeek.com/ (test on various mobile devices)

SECTION: SECTION: TESTING FOR SPEED
http://tools.pingdom.com (speed testing tool)
https://developers.google.com/speed/pagespeed/insights/ (speed testing tool)
http://gtmetrix.com (speed testing tool)
http://www.gidnetwork.com/tools/gzip-test.php (Gzip compression test)
http://jscompress.com/ (This tool compresses Javascript)
http://htmlcompressor.com/ (This tool compresses HTML code)
http://www.whatsmyip.org/http-compression-test/ (Test site's compression code)
https://developers.google.com/speed/docs/best-practices/payload?csw=1 (practices)

BECOME A WEBMASTER THAT SELLS
http://www.webmasterworld.com
http://www.ProBlogger.net
http://www.google.com/webmasters/tools (Google Webmaster Tools account)
http://www.bing.com/toolbox/webmaster (Bing Webmaster account)
https://www.google.com/analytics/

SECTION: MARKETING, PROMOTION & PUBLICITY
http://www.surveymonkey.com (create an online survey)
http://www.sitemaps.org
http://www.passionprofit.com/wts/sitemapgenerator.html (sitemap generator)
http://www.Submitnet.net (register your site with search engines)
http://www.addme.com (register your site with search engines)
http://www.prweb.com (submit press release)
http://www.PrLog.org (submit press release)
http://www.PR.com (submit press release)
http://www.TheOpenPress.com (submit press release)
http://www.IdeaMarketers.com (submit press release)
http://www.I-newsire.com (submit press release)
http://www.Newswiretoday.com (submit press release)
http://www.Free-Press-Release.com (submit press release)
http://www.24-7pressrelease.com (submit press release)

http://www.EcommWire.com (submit press release)
http://www.ezinearticles.com (submit articles)
http://www.findarticles.com (submit articles)
http://www.yahoogroups.com (submit articles)\
http://www.kickstarter.com/projects/1116206143/love-peace-and-sooouuuul-americas-favorite-dance-s (kickstarter campaign)
http://en.wikipedia.org/wiki/Comparison_of_crowd_funding_services
http://www.haro.com (Help a Reporter Out)
http://www.google.com/adwords
http://en.wikipedia.org/wiki/List_of_student_newspapers_in_the_United_States (student newspapers)

SECTION: SALES STRATEGY
http://www.saipanfactorygirl.com (bestseller)
http://www.discoverpagan.com (largest single transaction)
http://www.freesummerconcerts.com (donation model)

SECTION: YOUR MAILING LIST
http://www.passionprofit.com/wts/autoresponder (list management)
http://www.passionprofit.com/wts/autoresponder (autoresponder)
https://support.google.com/mail/answer/81126 (Bulk Senders Guidelines)

SECTION: BONUS CHAPTER ON BLOGGING
http://www.thesaipanblogger.com
http://www.welovesaipan.com (site Angelo and I started)
http://www.google.com/webmasters
http://www.Technorati.com (register your blog)
http://www.feedburner.com
http://www.Cafepress.com (merchandising store platform)
http://www.Sitemeter.com (tracker)
http://www.ExtremeTracker.com (tracker)
http://Problogger.net (for advice and tips for generating income as a blogger)

SECTION: MY NOT-SO-SECRET BUSINESS MODELS, IDEAS STRATEGIES
http://www.waltgoodridge.com/books (my ebook strategy)
http://www.discoversaipan.com (my tour guide strategy)
http://www.fastandgrowyoung.com (my public domain strategy)
http://www.cafepress/freesummer (my merchandising strategy)
http://www.zazzle.com (merchandising option)
http://www.freesummerconcerts.com (my donation/contribution strategy)

SECTION: OTHER STREAMS OF INCOME
http://www.google.com/adsense (advertising income)
http://www.textlinkbrokers.com (text link advertising income)
http://www.linkworth.com (text link advertising income)
http://www.ebay.com (sell your product)
http://www.elance.com (sell your services)

SECTION: EXPENSES
http://www.x-cart.com
http://www.1and1.com
http://www.powerpipe.com
http://www.efax.com
http://www.myfax.com/free/ (free fax service)
http://www.google.com/voice

SECTION: ONGOING DAILY ACTIVITIES
http://www.freeconferencecall.com (teleconferences)

SECTION: APPENDIX
    FAQ
http://www.nolo.com/encyclopedia/articles/sb/how_internet.html (choose domain)
http://realtytimes.com/rtnews/rtapages/20000105_domain.htm (choose a domain)
http://www.htmlgoodies.com (learn more about HTML)
http://www.esearch.com (internet research)
http://www.wilsonweb.com (newsletters and forums for webmasters)
http://www.problogger.net (newsletters and forums for webmasters)
http: www.webmasterworld.com (newsletters and forums for webmasters)
http://en.wikipedia.org/wiki/opt_in_e-mail (information on avoiding spamming)

    PENNY POWER MARKETING
http://www.saipanpreneur.com/archives/41/ (power of the penny)

    CASE STUDIES
http://www.saipanfactorygirl.com
http://www.hiphopbusinessplan.com
http://www.freesummerconcerts.com
http://www.happierabroad.com
http://www.globaltindahan.com
http://www.civilianside.com
http://www.gameslady.com

    A NOMADPRENEUR'S DREAM LIFE
http://www.jamaicanonsaipan.com

FINAL THOUGHT

How creating a website that sells can create a product that sells

An excerpt from *Websites That Sell (2014/2015 edition)* by Walt F.J. Goodridge author of *Turn Your Passion Into Profit*

Regardless of what type of product or service you wish to sell online, having a website that sells is vital to your success. All the preceding 262 steps apply to most every website, regardless of what type of product you're selling. However, here I'd share a little insight into my own creative process just for fellow authors and info-preneurs.

Coming up with a title

Typically, the title of the book/product is what hits me first. However, if all I have is a general idea of the subject matter, but don't yet have a winning title, I may spend time brainstorming. I won't rush this step in the process because the right title can make or break a project. The right title can help organize my thoughts around a specific meme or catch phrase. The right title may determine the best domain name to register. I'll often lie on my back in bed with eyes closed and meditate about a title. I'll walk on the beach in the early morning and just wait for the synapses in my brain to put certain concepts and ideas together to come up with the right combination of words for the title. Some of the actual titles I've used for my and clients' books include *Fast & Grow Young, From Bugle Boy to Battleship, The Tao of Wow, Change the Game, Chicken Feathers and Garlic Skin, Fit to Breed, and of course, Turn Your Passion Into Profit*! (Yes, I was the first to ever use this as a book title in 1999!)

I start with how I'll sell it

For me, along with the title, the product becomes real when the website exists. Therefore, the very first thing I do when I get a new idea for a book or info-product is create the webpage for it. Something magical happens when I can see the book in 3D form on a webpage. The book becomes real. This wasn't always the case. When I first started writing books (before the age of the internet), I would create a physical 3D mockup of my book. I'd find an actual published book that was the same size and page count as my intended book, and I would create a cover and wrap it around the book as a physical representation of my intended book. These days, I don't need to do that. After having written 30 books and a dozen info-products (some of which I've never actually held in physical form), the webpage and 2D/3D cover image are enough to bring the product to life! It will be just a matter of time before it exists either in digital or physical form for purchase.

I start with the headline, then I might write "Why I Wrote This Book," "What this book contains" (the features), and then start listing "What This Book Will do For You" (the benefits). It's in the process of ironing out this list of features and benefits (in other words, how I'll "sell" it), that the book essentially writes itself. Non-fiction writing is logic-based, process-oriented and results-driven. In other words, if I'm writing a book on how to start a record label, there is a certain process that I've executed (actually starting a label) that dictates the content of my book, a specific logical order that dictates the sequence of the steps of that process, and an agreed-upon outcome that those steps are required to achieve. (On the other hand, writing a fictional story is entirely different, and not my personal strong suit). My only challenge is simply to be as thorough, detailed and specific as I can be in recalling, documenting, organizing and presenting that process in my books.

As I create that webpage that sells, the product I'm selling is coming to life. The "Why I Wrote This Book" and the "What This Book Will Do For You" will become the introduction, and parts of it will be used for the press release. The "What This Book Contains" list of features and benefits will become the table of contents. I'm actually writing a book that sells at the same time that I'm creating the website that sells!

As I create that webpage, I am very aware that the soul of the book is being captured in the words, layout and design! This is what the world will see. This webpage and sales copy will be the first impression of the book the world will experience. What I say on this page is what will compel the world to place an order. This is what can generate income even before the book is actually finished. There've been many times that I've created a website sales page, upload it to the web, and have received purchases even before the book was written!

That's how creating a website that sells can actually help you create a product that sells!

For more insights, including 197 ideas, techniques, strategies, tips and tools for creating a money-making website, check out the Turn Your Passion Into Profit "Websites That Sell" Manual, available at http://www.passionprofit.com/store

###

Walt F.J. Goodridge is the author of *Turn Your Passion Into Profit, Living True to Your Self,* and *Ducks in a Row??? Please. How to find the courage to finally QUIT your soul-draining, life-sapping, energy-depleting, freedom-robbing job now...before it's too late..and live passionately ever after!* Discover his PassionProfit Philosophy and Formula, download 3 free ebooks, and take the Free Passionpreneur Personality Test at http://www.passionprofit.com

CONCLUSION

Ok. So there you have it. The best information I have for creating a website that sells. As I write this conclusion, upon waking up, it's now 7am on a Wednesday morning and I've already earned $224.

1) $122 from some text link ads
2) $ 35 from a site that sells my products (drop ship agreement)
3) $ 50 deposit (coaching client who clicked from an affiliate link)
4) $ 19 sale of the Websites That Sell ebook; this book you're reading

This gives some insight into what works and what doesn't when it comes to creating websites that sell.

Item 1 is what I call invisible income, revenue generated simply by placing a link on my sites. (sent to me via Paypal)

Item 2 is passive income. This partner website does its own advertising and marketing, takes the orders, Paypal's me the wholesale amount, and I ship the physical product to the customer.

Item 3 is consulting income. This individual completed a coaching questionnaire, then used the shopping cart to place a deposit on a coaching session. According to a notice I receive from ClixGalore, she found out about me from a link on an affiliate's website. So that affiliate earns a percentage of the deposit and any future revenue generated through that client.

Item 4 is residual income for an ebook. The shopping cart automatically fills the order, so I never have to mail a physical copy of the manual.

Items 5,6,7,8 and 9? At the same time other sites which I manage or with whom I have profit-sharing agreements might also be making sales at this very moment, but I won't receive that money until the end of the month as per a typical agreement.

The most important lesson I've learned in creating websites that sell is that things change. Strategies which worked a year ago, may not work today.

There was a time when advertising through Google's Adwords program was cost effective for my hiphopbiz products. As the field got a more crowded, and others started offering business products for the same market, the keywords I was bidding on became more expensive. Therefore, I no longer advertise those products through Google.

The majority of my site's traffic now comes from my top ten and top 20 positions in the regular search listings. Having been around for a few years now and accumulating links from other sites has put me in a good position. This does not mean that advertising through Google is no longer a viable strategy. It depends on your pricing and the keyword searches that you are targeting.

SUMMARY

In summary, I've found the following to be viable income streams:
• Direct product sales through my own site
• Sales through Amazon.com
• Orders directly from retail stores and wholesalers (Barnes & Noble, Baker & Taylor, et.al.)
• Placements on, and partnerships with other sites
• Text Link Ad Income (Adsense, Text Link Brokers, etc.)
• Ancillary Income Streams (Consulting, Speaking engagements, Teleclasses, Freelance Writing)

And that's what works for me!

*****

So there you have it! My best tips as well as THOUSANDS of dollars in savings using the vendors and methods I recommend above. With the right product, the right price, the right promotion, the right promotion and the right online presence and payment structure, there's absolutely no reason that you can't turn your passion into profit through a website that sells!

--Walt Goodridge
p.s. Any questions? Yes, you in the blue top.

APPENDIX

FREQUENTLY ASKED QUESTIONS

Getting Online FAQ

Q: Any tips for choosing a domain name?

A: Whenever I start a new project, one of the first things I do is think of an appropriate domain name. My idea is never really complete unless I have the "best" domain name. I must have the .COM version of a domain or I don't give the idea the green light. Don't let anyone fool you, it's still a .COM world.

If the marketing of the product is going to be strictly pay-per-click, for example if I'm marketing strictly through paid ads on Google, then I may use a less-than-optimal domain name since in this case, the actual website address is secondary. (eg. for the pay-per-click marketing of my book, Change the Game, I went with www.changethegamebook.com instead of the more desirable www.changethegame.com [someone else had it]).

If the marketing of the product or concept is going to rely heavily on word-of-mouth, then I'll hold out for a catchy .COM which says exactly what I wish it to say (eg. WeLoveSaipan.com).

With that said, you should choose a domain name that:

(a) reflects what your product does. If you're selling a product that helps people lose weight, for example, you may choose LoseWeight.com, WeightLossSecrets.com

(b) reflects how people know you or your product even if not grammatically correct

(c) reflects how people may search for your product in a search engine

(d) avoids ambiguity or confusion. Choose words that everyone knows how to spell. (Another thing I've learned is that people can't spell.) Is it i before e? Is there an e at the end of that word? Is that one "s" or two? Is that the number "1" or the word "one?"

(e) avoids being a "dot.net." If your ideal "dot.com" does not exist, choose something else. Tip: Names will sometimes become available when the current owner fails to renew ownership for the next year. If you are prepared to monitor its availability until it falls back into circulation, you might be able to secure your ideal name at some point in the future.

(f) avoids having letters in your domain name that may not be heard clearly over the phone or radio. Did she say "f" as in "frank" or "s" as in "Sam?" Did she say "d" as in "David" or "t" as in Tom?

Here is an example of someone who decided to go from a boring fact/feature type domain name (essupplements.com) to more memorable benefit, emotional-type one (JoeMuscle.com)...Keep this sort of thinking in mind as you think about ways to improve your own website's attractiveness to the public.

A search at your favorite search engine using terms such as "choosing a domain name", "how to choose a domain" etc, should reveal some good results of articles with tips. Here are two articles I found through google.com
http://www.nolo.com/encyclopedia/articles/sb/how_internet.html
http://realtytimes.com/rtnews/rtapages/20000105_domain.htm

Q: What if I already have a domain name?
A: That's GREAT! You can always have more than one domain name "pointing" to the same site. For example, both my www.hiphopentrepreneur.com, and my www.hiphopbiz.com domain names take visitors to the same site. Having different domain names allows you to experiment to discover which one is easier for people to remember and which one may lend itself to unique marketing ideas.

Q: If I have more than 1 domain, should I have multiple pages?
A: That's not necessary, based on the answer to the previous question. However, if each page has a different content and different key word meta tags, it might prove helpful in securing multiple placement in search engines.

Q: What if someone owns the domain name I want?
A: Find another one. If you brainstorm long enough, you can come up with something that suits you perfectly. But, here's a tip: just because someone currently owns your desire domain name, doesn't mean you can't have it soon. If someone owns your domain name, but hasn't put up a site yet, they may not really have plans to.

Consequently, the current owner may let his/her ownership lapse by not renewing ownership with the registrar. When you check on the ownership using networksolutions.com's "WhoIs" Database, make note of the "record expires" date. It it's scheduled to expire in a few weeks or months, you might get lucky and be able to grab it if they don't renew. That's what happened to me: now I own HIPHOPBIZ.COM after the original owner failed to renew, AND, now someone else owns BOB-MARLEY.COM when I failed to renew back in 1997 when I reserved it. But, whatever you do, DO NOT, I repeat, DO NOT notify the current owner that you're interested in the domain name, unless you DESPARATELY, REALLY want it and are willing to pay them for it now that they know it now has value to you!

Q: Will this manual help if I already have my business online?
A: YES. Your success on the web is a function of how many people know about you. The newspapers editor contact lists, ad swap sites, internet traffic reports, generic emails, and promotion techniques can all help you even if you're already online.

Q: Where can I learn more about HTML?
A: Try www.HTMLGoodies.com

Psychology of Internet Selling FAQ

Q: Why do people abandon their shopping carts?
A: Here is some research from esearch.com:

Why people most often abandon online transactions, from a survey of approximately 1,000 consumers (Since each respondent could mark more than one reason, the percentage will not total 100 percent.)

41% The Web page was too slow
20% The Web page looked unprofessional
16% The site didn't take credit cards
14% Couldn't find the check out area
12% Couldn't find a return policy
Source: Esearch

Q: What can I do to increase my online sales?
A: As I've said, provided your product or service has real value, the key to making more sales depends on you (1) saying the right thing, using the right words to say it, and instilling confidence in your customers that they will receive what they expect, and that they can purchase it securely and safely.
Here are some tips:

(a) Duplicate the winners. Check out what sites like Amazon.com, Dell and other sites that you KNOW FOR SURE are making money, and see how they design their pages, as well as how they structure their checkout and ordering process. Notice where they place their guarantee statements, privacy statements, pictures, white space. Remember, sometimes the simplest thing like where you place your "click here to order" link, may have an effect on your sales. So pay attention and follow the leaders.

(b) Join newsletters and participate in forums like those at
www.wilsonweb.com,
www.problogger.net
www.webmasterworld.com

(c) Talk to your customers to find out what is needed or wanted

Q: How can I avoid being accused of spamming?
A: Every now and then, I'll send a mailing to my list and receive complaints from my subscribers who may even report me as a spammer. To avoid this, please adhere to the following guidelines.

1. confirmed opt-in: exclusively send e-mails to recipients who subscribed and then confirmed that they solicit to receive advertising e-mails from you. See further information on http://en.wikipedia.org/wiki/opt_in_e-mail

2. one-click-unsubscribe: each of your e-mails should provide a link permitting the unsubscription via one single click. All other unsubscription methods that require the insertion of the e-mail address or a reply-message are not applicable.

3. text-format: always complement html-format by txt-format to assure that all of your recipients get your e-mails in a readable format.

4. indicate subscription: indicating where the recipient subscribed to your service shows him your e-mail is solicited and will 'refresh' his memory.

5. delete invalid addresses: give consideration to the bounce messages you receive. Automatically delete every address from your database for which you receive a bounced message.

Q: What can I do to increase my company's credibility?
A: Great question! There are, in fact, a set of guidelines offered by the Stanford Web Credibility Project.

Stanford Web Credibility Project

1. Make it easy to verify the accuracy of the information on your site.
You can build web site credibility by providing third-party support (citations, references, source material) for information you present, especially if you link to this evidence. Even if people don't follow these links, you've shown confidence in your material.

2. Show that there's a real organization behind your site.
Showing that your web site is for a legitimate organization will boost the site's credibility. The easiest way to do this is by listing a physical address. Other features can also help, such as posting a photo of your offices or listing a membership with the chamber of commerce.

3. Highlight the expertise in your organization and in the content and services you provide.
Do you have experts on your team? Are your contributors or service providers authorities? Be sure to give their credentials. Are you affiliated with a respected organization? Make that clear. Conversely, don't link to outside sites that are not credible. Your site becomes less credible by association.

4. Show that honest and trustworthy people stand behind your site.
The first part of this guideline is to show there are real people behind the site and in the organization. Next, find a way to convey their trustworthiness through images or text. For example, some sites post employee bios that tell about family or hobbies.

5. Make it easy to contact you.
A simple way to boost your site's credibility is by making your contact information clear: phone number, physical address, and email address.

6. Design your site so it looks professional (or is appropriate for your purpose).
We find that people quickly evaluate a site by visual design alone. When designing your site, pay attention to layout, typography, images, consistency issues, and more. Of course, not all sites gain credibility by looking like IBM.com. The visual design should match the site's purpose.

7. Make your site easy to use--and useful. We're squeezing two guidelines into one here.
Our research shows that sites win credibility points by being both easy to use and useful. Some site operators forget about users when they cater to their own company's ego or try to show the dazzling things they can do with web technology.

8. Update your site's content often (at least show it's been reviewed recently).
People assign more credibility to sites that show they have been recently updated or reviewed.

9. Use restraint with any promotional content (e.g., ads, offers).
If possible, avoid having ads on your site. If you must have ads, clearly distinguish the sponsored content from your own. Avoid pop-up ads, unless you don't mind annoying users and losing credibility. As for writing style, try to be clear, direct, and sincere.

10. Avoid errors of all types, no matter how small they seem.
Typographical errors and broken links hurt a site's credibility more than most people imagine. It's also important to keep your site up and running.

CONSUMER REPORTS WEBWATCH GUIDELINES

We believe Web sites will promote Web credibility if they adopt these basic policies:

Identity:
Web sites should clearly disclose the physical location where they are produced, including an address, a telephone number or e-mail address.

Sites should clearly disclose their ownership, private or public, naming their parent company.

Sites should clearly disclose their purpose and mission.

Advertising and Sponsorships:
Sites should clearly distinguish advertising from news and information, using labels or other visual means. This includes "in-house" advertising or cross-corporate ad sponsorships. Search engines, shopping tools and portals should clearly disclose paid result-placement advertising, so consumers may distinguish between objective search results and paid ads.

Sites should clearly disclose relevant business relationships, including sponsored links to other sites. For example: A site that directs a reader to another site to buy a book should clearly disclose any financial relationship between the two sites.

Sites should identify sponsors. The site's sponsorship policies should be clearly noted in accompanying text or on an "About Us" or "Site Center" page.

Customer Service:
Sites engaged in consumer transactions should clearly disclose relevant financial relationships with other sites, particularly when these relationships affect the cost to a consumer.

Sites should clearly disclose all fees charged, including service, transaction and handling fees, and shipping costs. This information should be disclosed before the ordering process begins.

Sites should clearly state and enforce policies for returning unwanted items or canceling transactions or reservations.

Corrections:
Sites should diligently seek to correct false, misleading or incorrect information.

Sites should prominently display a page or section of the site where incorrect information is corrected or clarified.

Sites should strive to mark content with its published date when failing to do so could mislead consumers.

Sites should clearly state their policy on a consumer's rights if a purchase is made based on incorrect information on the site.

Privacy:
Site privacy policies should be easy to find and clearly, simply stated.

Sites should clearly disclose how personal data from site visitors and customers will be used. Personal data includes name, address, phone number and credit card number.

Sites should disclose whether they use browser-tracking mechanisms such as "cookies," and other technologies such as Web beacons, bugs and robots.

Sites should explain how data collected from them will be used.

Sites should notify customers of changes to privacy policies, and provide an easy opt-out alternative.

The Final Words FAQ

Q: What if I have more questions?
A: You may wish to consider signing up for a consultation session with me at www.passionprofit.com/

Q: How else may I contact you?
A: You may contact me at: walt@passionprofit.com

WEB COPY SAMPLE

Here is a sample of how using the Web Copy Questions can help provide the content for your website. It's for a fictional product by George and Lora.

Why did you create this product?

We created this manual to help hopeful immigrants apply for and successfully get improved status in the United States!

What problem does the product solve, and for whom?

The Welcome to America 101 Guide can improve your chances of success applying for a Permanent Resident Status "Green Card." It was written for US citizens and their non-citizen spouses whether male or female. If your current or future husband or wife is a non-resident citizen of another country, and you dream of having her/him be a permanent resident of the US, this manual is for you!

How long has the product been selling steadily, and why?

Since its initial publication in 2012, and with each revision, this manual has helped thousands because it works!

What uses is the product especially appropriate for?

It is especially appropriate for military men whose overseas brides are eager to share in the American dream!

Where would you normally find one of its ingredients or components being used?

The interview tips in Chapter 4 are invaluable! The interview process is the most important part of the green card process. What you'll learn in this section may mean the difference between approval and denial.

What doesn't the product have, which makes it superior?

Unlike other books of, Welcome to America 101 doesn't have a lot of legalese and government-speak to confuse you. It's written in simple English by an average person who went through the process. It also includes case studies, interviews with others who've done it.

Nothing speaks like results. As a result of what they'll share with you, Lora is now a permanent resident of the United States, with a valid green card, free to travel anywhere she pleases, and with all the benefits that entails. Her next goal is full citizenship.

It's a cross between a what and a what?

Owning this manual is like having George as your best friend, sharing with you the actual forms he and Lora submitted, and offering personal tips and advice that the government could never legally or appropriately share with you. It's like having him as your coach mapping out a proven strategy.

How will the user feel when using it?

"We know how you feel. The green card process can be confusing and intimidating. I felt the same way. But after going through it, I found that while it may be tedious, it IS doable. I did it. We did it! You'll feel as empowered as we do now, and more confident about your chances of success than ever before. You'll have the insights and information, and a step-by-step plan to actually achieve what others do each year."—George & Lora

What does this product go well with?

This manual is the perfect supplement to the information on the USCIS.gov website.

What kind of testing went into making the product?

This manual has passed the most vital test of all: We used this information to get Lora her green card. It works!

Why is the price so reasonable?

Unlike most other manuals, we don't have a huge company to support. We don't hide the fact that all the information is available on the uscis.gov website. At only $27 for the ebook, $29.95(plus shipping) for the paperback, and with a money-back guarantee, it's well worth the investment and practically a risk-free endeavor to start your dream life applying for US permanent resident status.

Why might you want more than one product?

Order a paperback edition for your partner overseas and one for yourself. (we'll ship both to you, or split your order and ship one to your overseas spouse.)

Penny Power Marketing

A friend of mine recently started blogging and, in his first few days, earned 48 cents through pay-per-click ads. "Forty-eight cents???" you ask. Yes, forty-eight cents! But before you start laughing, answer this question:

Which would you rather have: a penny doubled each day for a month or $10,000? If you haven't already encountered this question before, you might be tempted to take the $10,000. After all, $10,000 is $10,000, and a penny is only a penny, right? Even if they suspect that doubling a penny each day might result in a huge number, most people might not intuitively realize just how much is really at stake. Well, the correct answer—provided you want the option that will make you richer—is to take the penny option. Here's what you will receive each day for 30 days if you do:

On Day 1 – You receive 1 cent
Day 2 - 2 cents
Day 3 - 4 cents
Day 4 - 8 cents
Day 5 - 16 cents
Day 6 - 32 cents
Day 7 - 64 cents
Day 8 - $1.28
Day 9 - $2.56
Day 10 - $5.12
Day 11 - $10.24
Day 12 - $20.48
Day 13 - $40.96
Day 14 - $81.92
Day 15 - $163.84
Day 16 - $327.68
Day 17 - $655.36
Day 18 - $1,310.72
Day 19 - $2,621.44
Day 20 - $5,242.88
Day 21 - $10,485.76
Day 22 - $20,971.52
Day 23 - $41,943.04
Day 24 - $83,886.08
Day 25 - $167,772.16
Day 26 - $335,544.32
Day 27 - $671,088.64
Day 28 - $1,342,177.28
Day 29 - $2,684,354.56
Day 30 - $5,368,709.12

Seen for what it is, this example is truly astounding! A single penny, doubled for an entire month yields a final day's payout of over 5 million dollars, AND a total accumulated payoff of over 10 million! It's an example of growth which progresses not arithmetically (i.e. by single units) but by what's known as "geometric progression. It's also called a geometric sequence or a geometric series-a sequence of numbers where each term after the first is found by multiplying the previous term by a fixed number called the "common ratio." Like the progression of rewards on the popular game show "Who Wants To Be A Millionaire," which starts at $100 and grows to a $1 million payoff in just 12 questions, by roughly doubling each prize (common ratio=2), the concept of geometric growth is indeed a powerful one.

But enough math. How does this apply to your business as a passionpreneur? Well, you can apply the principle of the doubling penny in your marketing and advertising to sell more products and grow your business.

However, before you get too excited, keep in mind that the reason many people never realize the full potential of their marketing and advertising efforts is simply this: They don't have the patience to see it through to the final payoff! Look back at our penny example for a moment, and notice how slowly the rewards seem to grow. A week after you've started, your daily take is still just 64 cents. Fifteen days later-fully half way through the process-your daily take is just $163, just 0.00305 percent of what it will be on the final day. (That's LESS than 1/2 of 1/10 of 1 percent!) Two-thirds of the way through at day 20, your payoff is $5242.88, just about 1/10 of a percent of what the reward will be on the final day. So for many people, unable to gauge how the momentum of a marketing campaign is really growing, abandon it before reaching the equivalent of their "Day 30" payoff.

Now imagine if the numbers in our penny example represented the number of people who bought your product. Or, let's be conservative, and say it represents the number of people who merely HEAR about your product. And let's say that only 1 percent of these people purchase your product for $25. That's 53,687 people x $25 = sales of $1,342,177.25.

Success in marketing is really a numbers game. The more people you tell, the more people become your customers. Do not be discouraged by what appears to be a small start and small rewards. Once you launch your business using the Quick Start Formula, and create a website that sells, continued persistence in your day by day efforts will eventually pay off!

For the full article, "The Power of the Penny" visit my article archives at http://www.saipanpreneur.com/archives/41/

A True Story of Buyer's Remorse

Even after you've branded yourself correctly, created a winning website, launched your *Penny Power* marketing campaign, tweaked your site and even made your first sale…it may too soon to celebrate! Yes, sometimes making the sale is not necessarily the end of the sales process! Let me share a recent true story with you.

A few weeks ago, at about 6:46pm EST on a Thursday, "Larry" purchased a paperback copy of Turn Your Passion Into Profit™. He had experienced difficulty using the log-in feature of the shopping cart when first attempting to purchase, so I had to interact with him briefly just before his purchase. So, when I saw his order successfully completed, I sent the following:

~~~~~~~~~~~~~~~~~~~~~~

Date: Friday March 19, 2010; 8:50am ChST = Thursday, 6:50pm EST
hey Larry,
Everything went through ok.
We'll get on this right away.
May I ask how you heard
about the book?--Walt

~~~~~~~~~~~~~~~~~~~~~~

The next day, Larry replied:

Saturday, March 20, 2010: 1:51pm ChST = Friday, 11:51pm EST
hell'o walt,
glad that my order finally went through but p[lease give me something a little more specific than we'll get on it right away. when can I expect my book to go out and how will it be shipped? Looking forward to your response being as timely as your advertising since you've already collected my money.   Thanks

A few minutes later, he sent another email:

Saturday, March 20, 2010: 2:03pm = Saturday, 12:03AM EST
Walt.....Just noticed an extra $5 fee added to the cost of my book that was not there when I placed my order. I'm going to trust that you will get back to me quickly on this as I'm starting to get a not so good feeling about this whole transaction. And please again....what does "at the first possible opportunity" mean when referring to my shipping date. Any chance of undoing this whole thing? Larry

An hour and twenty minutes later, I responded:

~~~~~~~~~~~~~~~~~~~~~~~

March 20, 3:20pm ChST = Saturday, 1:20AM EST
Larry,
I know how you feel. I felt the same way when I first
started ordering online.
Rest assured, however, that we've been in business since 1992
and online since 1997, and have served thousands and thousands
and thousands of customers. You will not find ANY sort of complaint about us on
any consumer site or in any Better Business Bureau records in all that time.
As it says on the transaction confirmation (which you provided), the $5 is a
shipping fee which, if you go back through the order process, and look closely, is
clearly and visibly indicated during the checkout process. (We haven't changed
anything in 10 years.)

FYI: We never see your credit card information, so VISA/MC only charge you
what you agree to on the shopping cart.

Your book has already shipped out to you from our
fulfillment center. I can't provide an EXACT arrival date (tracking would cost us
and you extra), but it is going by United States Postal Service mail, and already
out as I said, so it will likely be in the next 7 days.
~~~~~~~~~~~~~~~~~~~~~~~

March 20, 8:26pm ChST = Saturday, March 20, 6:26am EST
Thank you Walt for your timely response. However ,I've been ordering online for
years. That's probably the reason for my skepticism. Be looking forward to
receiving it.--   Larry

   So, here's what stands out to me about this exchange. From the very beginning,
Larry was receiving personalized attention from me. (99% of my customers
complete their book orders without speaking directly with the author of the book!)
        I can't recall anyone in the 18 years I've been selling via mail order, or the
10 years I've been selling online, who has questioned the "mysterious" shipping
charge. I wanted to ask Larry what planet he'd been living on, but decided to use a
variation of the "feel, felt, found" approach to setting him at ease (i.e. "I know
how you feel. I felt the same way. Here's what I found..")
        Larry still felt "buyer's remorse" and wanted to cancel his order, even
though he was speaking with a live person through the entire process.
        It wouldn't surprise me if, later, Larry asks for a refund.

        There are other subtleties embedded in the exchange that would provide
endless commentary for a customer service specialist. And, I'm sure there are

things I could have done better. My point is, simply, that I still had to work at having the sale "stick" even after the purchase.

At least one lesson we can draw from this is: Be specific in delivery dates and what happens next in the process to put people at ease.

Of course, 99% of your interactions will NOT be like this, but be prepared for that one in a hundred! All of which brings me to a few things I've learned about people.

A few things I've learned about people
In all my years in business, I've learned a few things about people that help me make sales, create good karma, and grow my business. Here are just a few that may help you with your website that sells!

(a) People are busy. Don't expect that they have time to read everything that you've spent time putting on your webpage. Therefore,

(b) People don't fully read their emails or all the great, valuable information you've painstakingly placed on your websites. You may have to repeat certain information several times even though it is clearly visible on your site or in your emails.

(c) People don't share the same level of technical expertise. There are still many new people who don't know how to send an email, or who will write their email addresses as www.walt@passionprofit.com or some strange variation of this.

(d) People want it "now." If they can't get it now, they'd like it sooner than later. So, if your product is normally delivered in three days, advertise that it will take five. That way they'll be surprised when it comes sooner.

(e) People live in fear. They suspect that you are an online scam artist.
Anything you do to allay those fears will help build trust and sales. (See "A True Story of Buyer's Remorse" in the appendix)

(e) People think that money is the most important thing for you, too. Let them know that you are not starving for their business, will gladly give refunds, and may even refuse their business for a given reason.

BONUS: CASE STUDIES OF WEBSITES THAT SELL

"All of these sites have the distinction of generating money on a consistent basis. They are all websites that sell and include my analysis of why they sell!"

www.saipanfactorygirl.com
Sweatshops are a hot topic. Personal diaries into hidden aspects of society and new cultures are intriguing.

www.hiphopbusinessplan.com
Hip Hop music is popular, and those who wish to be successful within that industry are numerous!

www.freesummerconcerts.com
FreeSummerConcerts is a unique site. It's a website that sells—not in the traditional sense—but it is a money-generator for contribution income. It serves a simple need the consumer has to get information compiled and presented in an easily-digestible format.

www.happierabroad.com
There are many men (and women) in the US in particular who are frustrated by the dating scene.

www.globaltindahan.com
The site owner is Filipino and knows his market. He knows what sells to Filipinos who live outside of the Philippines.

www.civilianside.com
One of the major challenges returning veterans face is securing employment.

www.gameslady.com
(see bonus article below)

BONUS ARTICLE:
WHY ISN'T MY WEBSITE MAKING MONEY

Why Isn't My Website Making Money????

A few weeks ago I took on a client and offered to help boost her sales by redesigning her website. With her previous design, which had been up for several months, she had garnered no sales. We began our experiment, and within a short period of time started receiving positive feedback from visitors, an increase in mailing list subscriptions, and ultimately, her first sales!

Barbara Sher is a Saipan, CNMI (Commonwealth of the Northern Mariana Islands) resident and author who creates games to help children have fun learning. She is written eight books and recorded one CD/tape on activities for children. Her books have been translated into eight languages; Italian, French, Spanish, Chinese, Estonian, Arabic, Russian and Swedish. She has written numerous articles for publications such as Mothering Magazine, Advance magazine, U.K's Kindred Spirit and on-line zine Writers Grrls. She is also a recipient of the World Rehabilitation Fund's "International Exchange of Experts" fellowship.

Barbara's previous books were published by Jossey-Bass, a subsidiary of Wiley Books, whose brands include For Dummies, Frommer's, Cliffs Notes, Betty Crocker and J.K. Lasser. She's now exploring the self-publishing route I always advocate (see "The Case for Self-Publishing Walt's Way, Publishing Basics April 2009 Newsletter)

Today's article is a case study of Barbara's www.GamesLady.com website. I'll interview Barbara herself in a future "Saipanpreneur Profile."

A FEW SECRETS

Here are a few of the things we did to help make Gameslady.com a website that sells. Of course, I can't reveal ALL my secrets, but these are a few of the obvious ones you can glean from actually visiting the site, and which I've used over the years to generate online sales for myself and my clients.

1. Lead with Testimonials

People follow people. The first thing you'll notice at gameslady.com is that we lead in with what others have said about Barbara's books and workshops. The power of testimonials cannot be overemphasized. Great testimonials, reviews and customer feedback are enough to sell just about anything. If you have limited time and space to make a pitch, focus on what respected authorities, as well as average people say about your product or service.

2. Simple long-form design

Rather than create a multi-layered website, I used a long-form style where all the information is presented on a single page. Boring? Perhaps. But quite effective. This keeps people from getting lost within the site.

Everything they need to know is right there, and all they have to do is scroll down to see. At the end of a long form site, you want people to do one or both of two things (a) place an order, (b) sign up to the mailing list.

3. Video of Barbara

People connect with people. In this case, as a woman selling games for children, I felt it was important to have people see and connect with Barbara, as a living, breathing person. So, I had Barbara film a short video right here on Saipan (no need for big production budgets, she used a regular digital camera), upload it to Youtube, and from there, I embedded it into the site. (Some of the first positive feedback she received, in fact, mentioned her "persuasive video presentation.")

4. Follow Webwatch Guidelines

There are other, more subtle things that have been incorporated that, in essence, build trust, establish credibility, encourage people to see the value in what is being offered, and most importantly feel safe in entering their credit card information to make a purchase.

Trusted consumer advocacy group, Consumer Reports, publishes what they call their "Webwatch Guidelines" a set of policies (for identity, advertising, customer service, and privacy issues) that they encourage all websites to incorporate to promote overall web credibility. Some of the Webwatch policies include:

• Web sites should clearly disclose the physical location where they are produced, including an address, a telephone number or e-mail address.
• Sites should clearly disclose their purpose and mission.
• Sites should clearly disclose all fees charged, including service, transaction and handling fees, and shipping costs. This information should be disclosed before the ordering process begins.
• Sites should clearly state and enforce policies for returning unwanted items or canceling transactions or reservations.
• Sites should clearly disclose how personal data from site visitors and customers will be used. Personal data includes name, address, phone number and credit card number.

These and other design elements are critical to online success.

A FEW IMPORTANT POINTS

It's always difficult to pinpoint exactly why a specific customer orders from a site. Is it the new design? Is it mainly the video? Were they referred by a trusted source? You'll likely have those questions, too.

During our experiment, Barbara had many suggestions and questions about how we were proceeding. So, in response to Barbara's (and your) questions about the specifics of online success, here are a few bits of advice, and observations from actual emails I sent to her.

1. Sometimes Less is More

"More is not necessarily better. There is an art to leaving enough UNSAID so as to encourage people to use their imaginations to make the sale (i.e. convince themselves to purchase) for themselves. If you've ever purchased from catalogs/mail order in the past–especially when you were a child–you might recall the thrill of having your mind work overtime imagining all sorts of things about your doll/book/dress/sea monkeys/pet rock based on just a few choice words and pictures in an ad. It's that sense of anticipation of "what's in store" that good sales copy evokes."

2. Everything is a Process

"Yes, those sales might have happened even if the site had not been redesigned. We'll never know, but what we DO know is that you didn't make ANY sales for the months the site was as it was before. Now the site is different, and you made sales. Coincidence, perhaps? Correlation doesn't equal causation, but even if the only purpose the new design served was to make you more proud of it, and thus more motivated to send your email announcement of your new book to your mailing list, the fact remains, it was part of the PROCESS that got us here—a process that has now begun."

3. Be Realistic About and Recognize Your Progress

"I remember reading an article many years ago that stated that something like 97% of websites on the internet NEVER make any money. Millions of people pay for/and/or build sites, create products, advertise, and wait, and NEVER make a single sale, EVER. Your new site has been up about 60 days, and you've already generated a growing mailing list and are making sales, putting you, whether you realize it or not, in the top 3% of sites worldwide. And, most significantly, those sales came right after you DID something to generate them, which brings us to..."

4. You Need to Be Doing More

"I read another article many years ago, as well, that likened people's expectations of internet profits to "building a store in a vast desert and wondering why no one is showing up to make them rich!"

"Your previous publisher makes sales because they are doing things to make those sales. They have an established reputation, good will, sales agents, advertising campaigns, relationships with sales outlets, an existing distribution channel, satisfied customers, and much more which make the sale of a thousand books a month quite an easy feat. You have a single store in the middle of a desert, with an average of 10 people a day visiting. All we've done up to this point, is simply change the design, and wait for people to find us. That's not enough. As a "newbie" self-published author, you should be

• sending out a weekly, or monthly email to your fan base/mailing list
• arranging interviews on radio
• registering your site with other directories
• visiting and posting on bulletin boards, blogs and chat rooms
• writing and promoting articles based on your expertise
• creating more Youtube videos and promoting them
• sending review copies to magazines, etc."

Yes, it's a bit more than simply "build it and they will come!"

FINALLY
The list of what it takes to make a website—especially a self-published author's website—truly sell goes on and on.
It is part art and part science. It involves intuition. It involves following rules. It differs from site to site. It changes based on the season, the product being offered and a hundred other factors. However, we were able to accomplish this for Barbara Sher's Gameslady.com. I hope some of what we learned in her case study will be useful to make your own website one of the few, one of the proud, and one of the profitable....websites that sell!"

SAMPLE PRESS RELEASE #1

"This is the actual press release I use each year for freesummerconcerts.com."

FOR IMMEDIATE RELEASE:

FREESUMMERCONCERTS.COM Announces 10th Year & 2014 Season of free concerts NATIONWIDE!
Once only for New Yorkers, free service now launches nationwide!

MAY 2014--Every summer, the nation's parks, piers, plazas and pathways host some of best musical entertainment in the world free to the public! From Rock, Jazz, Classical, R&B, Hip Hop, Country, Salsa and Reggae to Folk– an free, 8-year old online service helps residents and tourists stay on top of it all.

"Like many people, I was always hearing about free concerts I missed...usually a day later when everyone was talking about how much fun they had!" Goodridge explains, recounting how, in 2005, the idea for the site came to him. "So, one summer, I took the time to compile every event that was available here in New York, created a little computer program to email myself and a few friends reminders of what was happening each week. Word spread, and the rest, as they say, is history!"

The site, now enjoying its 10th summer season as the leading summer event aggregator in New York City, now boasts a calendar of over 1,600 events including Summerstage, Celebrate Brooklyn and the perennial Wingate Field and Seaside Concert series. It survives on a contribution strategy of contributions from a mailing list of loyal fans and followers–many of whom have been on board since the beginning.

Using that simple business model, Goodridge hopes to expand the service nationwide by employing a team of music mavens to franchise the concept for major metropolitan regions in each state!

Summer officially starts on June 21, but the FreeSummerConcerts fan base starts buzzing as early as January each year," Goodridge adds.

Learn more and Sign up at www.FreeSummerConcerts.com

###

SAMPLE PRESS RELEASE #2

"This is the actual press release we used for the launch of civilianside.com, featuring the book, Rucksack to Briefcase.

FOR IMMEDIATE RELEASE:

Rucksack to Briefcase. New guidebook helps military service members transition from deployment to employment

SUMMARY: A new guidebook by a twice deployed army Master sergeant turned corporate recruiter offers resume writing tips, job hunting strategies and interviewing techniques for military service members returning home in search of employment.

Sugar Land, TX--A new guidebook by a twice deployed army Master sergeant turned corporate recruiter, Dylan Raymond offers resume writing tips, job hunting strategies and interviewing techniques for military service members returning home in search of employment.

"It was a difficult and frustrating transition for me," says former Chief Warrant Office Raymond, who, after deploying to both Iraq and Kuwait returned home in search of a civilian job. "There was no practical training that prepared me for what I went through, and so I made a personal promise that when I eventually got back on my feet, that I would help other service members as much as I could."

Raymond, who also served for 4 1/2 years as field army recruiter, and now as a personnel recruiter for an offshore drilling company, has seen both sides of military transition.

"Military service and experience have no direct civilian-side equivalent to demonstrate to a private business owner how his bottom line will be affected by hiring you," he adds. "Therefore, the challenge is to develop a new language and 21st century strategy service members can use to translate that military experience and training into value that civilian employers can understand."

Rucksack to Briefcase includes sample resumes, case studies, Frequently Asked Questions, checklists and more and is available on Amazon.com

For chapter preview and to order in paperback and ebook formats, visit www.civilianside.com and contact Chief Raymond for interviews and review copies at questions@civilianside.com or (832) 301-5110

###

GLOSSARY

Condition formula: one of a set of proven strategies one can take to move the state of a given situation, project, business, or relationship from one state to a higher state of survival. The formulas names include "Non Existence," "Danger," "Emergency," "Normal," "Affluence," Power Change," and "Power," and are from the works of L.Ron Hubbard.

Domain: Your web address (eg. www.passionprofit.com) is known as a domain, or domain name.

FTP: File Transfer Protocol is the process by which the files that make up your website are uploaded and saved onto your hosting companies servers so that they can be accessed by people on the internet. You can use a program like "Fetch" (for Macs) or WSFTP (for PCs) to "ftp" your files.

HTML: Hyper-text Markup Language is the code that constitutes your web page. Next time you visit a website, click on "View→view source code," or right click on a blank space on the page and find the "view source" option and you will see what raw HTML code looks like.

merchant account: Setting up a merchant account allows you to accept and process credit cards from your customers.

Nomadpreneur: : n. a mobile entrepreneur able to generate income while free of the restraints of a physical location or business presence. A nomadpreneur has money and mobility.

non-existence: The condition formula of most importance to a new business or individual starting a new position or job.

Passion: a hobby, talent or interest.

Passionpreneur: someone who has use a passion as the basis of an entrepreneurial venture.

Product: a high quality object or service in the hands of a consumer in exchange for something of value. It is not a product if it has not been exchange for value.

SSL: Secure Socket Layer is a way for computers, web browsers and servers to communicate that keeps information encrypted, private and secure.

ABOUT THE AUTHOR

Short Version:

"Once upon a time, there was a frustrated civil engineer who hated his job, followed his passion, started a sideline business publishing his own books, found the courage to quit his job, ran away to a tropical island in the Pacific, and started tourism business so he could give tours of the island to pretty girls every day....and live a nomadpreneur's dream life!"

Long Version:

A Columbia University graduate with a Bachelor of Science degree in civil engineering, Walt Goodridge was, like many people, headed for a career in his profession of training. In fact, immediately after graduating, he accepted a job in the Design Division of the Port Authority of New York & New Jersey's Engineering department on the 73rd floor of World Trade Center One. However, within the first fifteen minutes of this his first job in corporate America, Walt realized beyond the shadow of a doubt, that he absolutely hated it!

It was several years until he was able to grow his sideline ventures-- starting with his personal passion in the music industry--and walk away from the monotony and restriction of nine-to-five employment to become a full-time "passionpreneur."

As he honed his expertise in website development, internet marketing, and in living true to himself, he developed the original Turn Your Passion into Profit™ Philosophy and Formula along with a coaching practice to help others do the same. In 1999, he published the formula in Turn Your Passion into Profit™ which, with yearly updates, has consistently sold in the top 50 in home-business books on Amazon.com.

A few years later, Walt booked a one-way ticket to an island in the Pacific, escaped the rat race to live out his dream of being a "nomadpreneur."

Walt currently owns and operates over 50 websites, has written over of 25 books and products, over 400 articles and over 500 inspirational poems called "Life Rhymes." He has been an artist manager, radio deejay, record label owner, inventor, poet, network marketer and consultant. He has written for Entrepreneur Magazine and Black Enterprise, and has been featured in Time Magazine, The Wall Street Journal Online, the Dallas Morning News, The Kip Business Report and numerous publications and websites.

Walt is originally from the island of Jamaica, and now lives a vegan lifestyle on the equally tropical island of Saipan in the Pacific.

You may contact Walt at P.O. Box 503991 Saipan MP 96950, or by calling (646) 481-4238, or via email at Walt@passionprofit.com.

APPENDIX: Suggested products in the PassionProfit™ Series
Collect the whole set! ☺

❏ *Turn Your Passion Into Profit™: A Step-by-Step Guide for Turning ANY Hobby, Talent, Interest or Product idea into a money-making venture!*
Discover the profit in your passion. Make money doing what you love!
Paperback: $24.95; Ebook: $16.95
ebook: http://www.passionprofit.com/store/product.php?productid=24

❏ The "Quick Start" Manual
I've launched business ventures and made sales in as little as 48 hours! Now you can achieve the same results by using this convenient step-by-step, action checklist! I'll share the methods, as well as the specific vendors, sites and software I use to get my own and my clients' operations up and running from idea to income as quickly as possible! Perhaps you'll beat my quick start record!
Paperback: $19.95 ; ebook: $16.00
http://www.passionprofit.com/store/product.php?productid=18

❏ *Turn Your Passion Into Profit 6-CD Audio Set Now Available!*
Turn Your Passion into Profit is now available as an audio series. Listen to Walt explain the entire passion to profit philosophy and formula. These six audio CDS include live workshops, coaching sessions and more.
CD: $49.95
cd: http://www.passionprofit.com/store/product.php?productid=20

❏ *The Tao of Wow & The Art of Wow*

Find your wow factor! Make the world go wow!

Paperback only: $16.95;

http://www.passionprofit.com/store/product.php?productid=22

You are reading this title:

☑ *The Websites That Sell Manual*

There is an art and a science to designing a website that communicates your value, heightens your credibility, inspires consumer confidence and compels visitors to whip out their credit cards and order your product or service online! There are some things you should NEVER do, and other things you absolutely MUST if you want to make money online.

Paperback: $19.95; Ebook: $16.95

ebook: http://www.passionprofit.com/store/product.php?productid=25

All titles and more are available at www.passionprofit.com/store

FREE EBOOKS AND ONGOING SUPPORT

"Join my PassionProfit mailing list at http://www.passionprofit.com/free and receive the following ebooks free of charge, and receive weekly information, inspiration and ideas to help you turn your passion into profit!"

❏ Get these FREE ebooks! ❏

All available free by joining the Turn Your Passion Into Profit™ mailing list at http://www.passionprofit.com/free

In Search of a Better Belief System

7 Conversations to Freedom

How to Become a Nomadpreneur

❏ Find me online ❏

See all of my books at www.waltgoodridge.com/books

❏ Read me online ❏

See an archive of (most of) my articles at www.saipanpreneur.com/archives

❏ Follow me online ❏

Facebook: http://www.facebook.com/passionprophet

Twitter: @whereiswalt

Nomad Blog: www.jamaicaninchina.com

A Nomadpreneur's Dream Life
(a prelude Nomadpreneur SECRETS)

The "Since You Asked" FAQ

Okay, you didn't ask, but here's a little incentive for you. The whole purpose of my own desire to create my own websites that sell was and continues to be FREEDOM!

I wanted the luxury of having streams of income that do not require my physical presence in any single location. In other words, I wanted the freedom to become a nomadpreneur and see the world with a constant source of income paying the bills. On Feb 23, 2006, I was able to accomplish that in a personally meaningful way. Here's the beginning of that story that I hope can inspire you to seek your own definition of happiness!

"Once upon a time, there was a civil engineer who hated his job, followed his passion, started a sideline business publishing his own books, made enough money to quit his job, ran away to a tropical island in the Pacific, and started a tourism business so he could give tours of the island to pretty girls every day!"

That's the story right there! In some similar form or another, all of us have (or should have) such a tale of aspiration, fulfillment and actualization we'd like to tell about ourselves. Let me share with you a few details of my own story.....

The Life I Live

I admit, there is a bit of a conundrum here. On one hand, my goal is to live a simple, minimalist, natural, vegan lifestyle, close to the land, far away from the hustle & bustle, negative influences, destructive lifestyle, and pollution of large, crowded, impersonal, industrial cities, and with minimal exposure to and influence from the brain draining, energy-depleting, mind-numbing, materialist-centered, consumer-driven distractions and disempowering agendas of the entertainment and news media. At the same time, recognizing my purpose to teach and help others in the search for truth, and my passion for writing and sharing information, I, therefore, have aspirations to achieve a greater reach for my products. This requires, to some degree, involvement in and interaction with others who are living the very lifestyle I wish to escape.

But, thanks to my websites that sell, I have the best of both worlds! I've created a business model that allows me to live the fringe lifestyle of my choosing, but which connects me to the mainstream in necessary ways. So, from here on a Pacific island, with just a laptop, an internet connection, a camera and a cell-phone, I can:

1. honor my passion doing the writing I enjoy, creating new books, CDs, and videos, writing my weekly column and other articles, etc.,

2. run my business launching new websites, testing and tweaking new marketing campaigns, fulfilling orders, dealing with customers, and still

3. reach the buying public and the media necessary to promote and sell my products. Through services like Skype and MrConference.com, or simply a telephone line, or email, I can conduct teleclasses and workshops, do coaching and consulting, answer inquiries, and even "appear" on media outlets to promote my products, and help others do the same!

And at the same time, when I want to, I can take the "office" out to the beach, or under the shade of a coconut tree and run things from there! Or, I can be a nomadpreneur and head off to China, Bali, Singapore, or Thailand, and as long as there's an internet connection, I can do it all from wherever I happen to be! Let me share with you how it all started….

Note 1: How it all Began

It was all just one of those seemingly spontaneous, but subconsciously orchestrated decisions, stemming from a set of seemingly random, but divinely engineered events that led to my seemingly fortuitous, but cosmically predictable arrival on the island of Saipan.

In December of 2005, my friend Ken, who lived in Las Vegas, Nevada at the time, happened to be in Brooklyn, New York visiting a friend. He invited me to a holiday party that was to take place on Saturday, December 16, 2005.

When that Saturday rolled around, I made the long, late night train ride from Harlem to Brooklyn. After the party ended, at about 3:00 a.m. or 4:00 a.m. that Sunday morning, I was all set to leave, when we discovered that Ken's car was blocked in by a neighbor's. Ken suggested we knock on the neighbor's door, and request that she let us out. However, rather than wake the neighbor up so early on a Sunday morning, I suggested we simply chat and wait it out, as the sleeping neighbor would likely be up in a few hours to go to church.

After touching on a few random topics, we happened to get into a discussion about Ken's recent trip to Japan to produce some music for some Japanese artists. While there, the artists took Ken to Saipan to work with a producer on that island.

He had such a wonderful time that he went back again several months later. He revealed the details of his "good time" to me that night in Brooklyn. Something about it piqued my interest, sparked my curiosity, and stirred my latent nomadic streak, which I had kept submerged for all these years.

The prospect of living life in a whole new world came at a time when, jaded by the materialism and crowded yet often isolated living of metropolitan life, I was seeking to reinvent myself. Ken's pitch contained all the right words and phrases: warm weather, beautiful people (read: women), slower lifestyle, all while still on the U.S. Postal System—a seemingly trivial, yet important consideration for my mail order business. Yes, something clicked, and I made a decision that night that I was Saipan-bound.

I bought my ticket, gave away my 2500-strong vinyl lp collection, donated my books to a combination of friends and street vendors, unloaded almost everything I owned, and jetted.

Two months after that fateful conversation, I executed my escape from America. The date was February 23, 2006.

I always think about the fact that had I not gone to that party that night, and had we not opted to wait out the wee morning hours engaged in conversation, that the topic of travel and Saipan may not ever have come up, and present Saipan as an option for this now quite happy nomadpreneur. Ahhh, yes. What mightn't have been.

But, let me go back a bit and fill in some of the details.

Note 2: Freedom Song

Yep, after Ken's pitch, I was all set to make a drastic change in my life. I started doing research, sending emails requesting information, making connections on couchsurfing.com, and booking fares and accommodations for the journey. As the day of my departure got closer, I sent the following email to a few friends, customers and clients:

February 9, 2006
hi all,

As you may have surmised, and as was hinted at in several of my recent Friday Life Rhymes (specifically #437 entitled "Freedom Song"), something's been brewing in "Walt World" for the past few months.

Ever since leaving corporate America in the fall of 1995, I've been executing a plan to create the lifestyle of a modern, minimalist, nomadic, passionpreneur based on a passive-residual income stream! In other words, I want out of the rat race!

Now that I've cut all the tethers and structured a turnkey, self-sustaining, internet-based business that doesn't require my physical presence in any one location......(drum roll, please)

...I've bought a one way ticket to the island of Saipan in the South Pacific! [note: Saipan is actually in the Western Pacific, but South sounds so much more exotic]

So amid sea, sand and sun, I'll be living my dream in a clime that resonates with who I wish to be.

Since this is the first step in a journey of a thousand smiles, I didn't want to make a big deal about it until I got there and surveyed the lay of the land. But, I wanted to tell a few friends and contacts who deserve a little advanced notice...

You can still reach me at walt@passionprofit.com, and I'll set up a Skype™ account and MSN Messenger for IMs for anyone who'd like to keep in touch, and share the experience!

Walt

p.s. I leave next Wed February 15 for Las Vegas, and then I'm on to Japan—my first stop on the way to Saipan! If you know of anyone there in Tokyo I can call who might be kind enough to show me around, please let me know. And in case you didn't receive Life Rhyme* #437, here it is again:

Freedom Song	One day you'll write about me:
One day you'll think about me:	There's the man who lived his dream
Haven't seen him in a while	Cut loose the oars and left the boat
You'll make a note to find me	to swim a different stream
or a number you can dial	
	And then one day amid the noise
One day you'll ask about me:	and hustle of the throng
Where on earth can he be found?	You'll hear a tune first faintly
And learn at last I've set my sail	that's been playing all along
where sun and sea abound	
	You'll know the singer instantly
One day you'll say about me:	you'll recognize my voice
Goes the nomad on his way	A heart-felt freedom song
To live the life's adventure	of life lived not by chance but choice...
that he said he would some day	[end of email]

And so began my escape from America. What follows is the real-time,

The Reality

It was very empowering and satisfying to be able to write and send that "Freedom Song" email and to actually embark on the journey of a lifetime. You can read the entire chronicle of my "escape" in Jamaican on Saipan, available at www.JamaicanonSaipan.com. Hopefully, it can inspire you to do something equally satisfying and fulfilling to honor your own dreams.

I am able to live my nomadpreneur dream life because, I use the information and strategies you now have available in this manual, to quick start my business ideas, and create "effortless income" through designing and promoting websites that sell!

Live true to your self and live your best life!
Walt F.J. Goodridge author of *Turn Your Passion Into Profit*™
The adventure continues *in Nomadpreneur SECRETS*..